AN OFFICIAL BEHIND-THE-SCENES COMPANION

RACHEL BERTSCHE

THE KICK-A** BOOK OF

COBRA KAI

DEYST.

An Imprint of WILLIAM MORROW

CONTENTS

INTRODUCTION

"COBRA KAI NEVER DIES"

For kids growing up in the 1980s, *The Karate Kid* was more than a movie. The 1984 film and its two sequels were hallmarks of a generation—they introduced phrases like "wax on, wax off," and "sweep the leg"; established "You're the Best Around" as the seminal movie montage anthem; created the prototype for the classic '80s bully in Johnny Lawrence (much more on this to come!); and cemented the ideals of wisdom and mentorship in the beloved Mr. Miyagi. The trilogy was not only a pop culture classic but a box office success: collectively, the first three films of the "Miyagi-verse" grossed more than $300 million worldwide. They also spawned a 1994 installment, *The Next Karate Kid* starring Hilary Swank, and a 2010 remake, also called *The Karate Kid*, starring Jaden Smith. In the decades since, its legacy has only grown: the internet hosts endless tributes and parodies, and parents—who were

Ralph Macchio Pat Morita

The
Karate Kid

kids when the original movie came out—now share it with their own children. It has somehow become fodder for nostalgic humor while remaining one of Hollywood's most sincere coming-of-age stories. Like most great art and entertainment, that is no accident.

Cobra Kai creators and executive producers Josh Heald, Jon Hurwitz, and Hayden Schlossberg were seven years old when The Karate Kid hit theaters in 1984. Heald and Hurwitz saw it on the big screen; Schlossberg on VHS not long after. By the time the three became friends (Hurwitz and Schlossberg met at Randolph High School in New Jersey; Heald, also a Jersey native, met Hurwitz when they were classmates at University of Pennsylvania), they'd each spent years with the films. "These were movies that we watched over and over again throughout our childhoods and our teenage years, and we constantly found new things to love about them," Hurwitz says. "By early college, we were obsessed with the Cobra Kai side of the story. We all love the underdog story of Daniel, and we loved the connection with Mr. Miyagi, but when you've seen it a zillion times and you're a huge comedy fan, you start to realize how hilarious it is that there was basically a karate gang terrorizing a high school. It was very different than the typical high school football player bully you usually see."

Schlossberg notes that once he gained perspective on what high school was *really* like, his childhood take on the movie shifted. "There are different approaches to The Karate Kid at different phases of your life," he says. "There's the initial one when you're a kid and you're connecting to the underdog story, and you get caught up in the emotion of it all. But then there's the post–high school years, when you're looking back and seeing it for the way it maybe *didn't* capture reality—at least the reality of how we lived our high school existences. The fact that the movie had bullies riding around on motorcycles with multicolored jackets, unleashing karate on the new kid, there was something about it that was kind of fun and funny in a heightened way."

The trio developed an appreciation for William Zabka, who seemed to be the go-to actor for high school villain roles in the '80s—not just in the *Karate Kid* films but also in 1985's *Just One of the Guys*, *National Lampoon's European Vacation*, and the 1986 Rodney Dangerfield hit, *Back to School*. Says Hurwitz, "We kind of leaned into the comedy of how ridiculous it was that William Zabka was playing this asshole in a bunch of movies—so much so that when I was in college and I learned how to make web pages, I had one dedicated to the New York Mets, one dedicated to a group of my high school friends, and one dedicated to 'William Zabka as '80s asshole.'" The fan page featured images, quotes, and tongue-in-cheek descriptions of each of the actor's bad-boy roles.

But it wasn't until all three friends had graduated from college and moved to Hollywood to write screenplays that they considered the idea that there was more to Johnny Lawrence's story. A special edition *Karate Kid* DVD came out in 2005, featuring an interview with William Zabka discussing his approach to

his now-classic role. "William said that in Johnny's mind, he wasn't a bully. In Johnny's mind, he was just another kid in high school, trying to make it work. He's trying to turn over a new leaf and then suddenly this new kid moves to town. And just as Johnny wants to mend fences with his girlfriend—his first love—the new kid gets in the way, and it led to this rivalry for him," Hurwitz says. "So William always approached the character not as a bully but as another kid in high school trying to get by, and hearing him talk about that inspired us to have conversations about the bullies from our own high schools and start to ask the questions: *What makes a bully? Does a bully think he's a bully? And what happens to a bully when he grows up?*"

Wouldn't it be amazing, Heald, Hurwitz, and Schlossberg wondered, to get the rights to *The Karate Kid* and make a movie called *Cobra Kai*? To see what happened to Johnny Lawrence all these years later? To take a bully that people all over the world know and finally do his story justice?

The idea was compelling, sure, but the reality of getting such a movie made seemed impossible. It was the mid-2000s, and the film industry was driven by franchises and star power. *The Lord of the Rings, Harry Potter,* and *Pirates of the Caribbean* movies were among the biggest box office draws, and audiences were flocking to comedies like *Wedding Crashers*, starring Bradley Cooper and Owen Wilson, and *Hitch* with Will Smith. Pitching a film with William Zabka and Ralph Macchio as the headliners—two actors who'd been hugely successful two decades earlier but were still known largely for their '80s roles— would be an uphill battle. So, the guys moved forward with other projects. Hurwitz and Schlossberg wrote *Harold & Kumar Go to White Castle* and its two sequels, and Heald wrote the 2010 comedy *Hot Tub Time Machine*. Still, as the years passed, the screenwriters took note of two new, significant developments in entertainment: long-form storytelling on up-and-coming streaming services, and TV shows centered around nostalgic, fan-favorite characters. "I remember the three of us driving down Sunset Boulevard and seeing a billboard for *Fuller House*," Hurwitz says. "We saw Kimmy Gibbler up there—someone you wouldn't typically see on a billboard, a star in the past or even just a minor character in the past—and we looked at each other and were like, '*The Karate Kid* is just as big as *Full House*, and Johnny Lawrence is just as big as

Kimmy Gibbler.' We decided to see if we could actually do *Cobra Kai*, but as a streaming series."

The guys got together—at Schlossberg's apartment ("it was our war room back then," says Heald) as well as his shared office with Hurwitz—to brainstorm what *Cobra Kai*, the TV series, might look like. The office that Hurwitz and Schlossberg shared was only blocks from where the Cobra Kai scenes were shot in the original *Karate Kid* films, which helped spark extra excitement around the idea. They started a story document, which they built upon each time they met. The earliest meetings focused on big story lines and major character creation—specifically the character of Miguel Diaz, who they knew would be integral to the plot—and the where-are-they-now of the movies' heroes and villains. Soon, an entire first season was fleshed out. "It was so much richer than what a movie would have been," Hurwitz says. "We had the real estate within a season not just to tell Johnny Lawrence's story but also to tell the Daniel LaRusso story in a thorough way, and to have a whole new generation of karate kids with their own unique stories."

Heald, Hurwitz, and Schlossberg plotted an entire first season, which would tell the story of a down-and-out Johnny Lawrence, now in his fifties, who takes his teenage neighbor under his wing, ultimately reopening the Cobra Kai dojo from his youth and becoming a sensei; and Daniel LaRusso, the now-successful owner of a car dealership chain, who has used his karate past to build his brand, but who is struggling to connect with his children and keep balance in his life after the death of his mentor, Mr. Miyagi. A brand-new cast of characters would join the expanded Miyagi-verse, but the through line would be a renewed rivalry between the two men, neither of whom are able to successfully put the past behind them.

The first step to getting the show made—before even writing a script—was securing permission from Overbook Entertainment, Will Smith's production company, which owned the rights to the *Karate Kid* franchise. "We knew that Overbrook did the Jaden Smith movie [the 2010 *Karate Kid* remake], but we didn't know if there was a real affection for the original *Karate Kid* films," Hurwitz says. "We went into our very first meeting super prepared, with all these strategies for how to sell Caleeb [Pinkett, president of Overbook], but it turned out he was just as big a *Karate Kid* fan as we were. The three of us talked for like forty minutes straight, sharing with Caleeb much of what viewers can now see in season one of the show, and he was just sitting there with a smile on his face, taking it all in. When we finished, he started rattling off what he liked about different story lines, referencing minor characters we'd mentioned in only one sentence half an hour earlier, and he was so invested in the story." Pinkett helped the trio get approval at Overbrook, and soon they got Sony Pictures Entertainment, who owned the *Karate Kid* intellectual property, to sign off as well.

"At that point, we knew what we had was undeniable," Heald says. "We'd been given permission to play within the *Karate Kid* universe, which to us was as valuable as if George Lucas had given us the keys to *Star Wars*. This was a fandom that we knew intimately and characters we knew how to write because we had never stopped talking about them." But, of course, nothing was going to happen without two very important players: William Zabka and Ralph Macchio. *Cobra Kai* would never happen if they couldn't sign on these two stars.

Luckily, Heald and Zabka had worked together on *Hot Tub Time Machine*, in which Zabka played Rick, *yet another* iteration of an '80s asshole. In the years since, the two had talked extensively about Johnny Lawrence. "I knew that William had some personal demons associated with playing that character and other '80s bad guys in his youth, with people coming up to him on the street and saying things like, 'Oh, you're that bad guy. You're such an asshole,'" Heald says. "The first hundred times it maybe rolls off your back, but a lifetime of that had taken its toll, to a degree. William had a desire, I think, to exorcise those demons and step back into the character, so we believed that bringing him Johnny Lawrence, who we now had the permission for him to inhabit, would be a gift. Plus, we were introducing brand-new territory for this character. We weren't rehashing the past, we were dramatizing someone who was a bit one-dimensional in the movies."

While Zabka had thought about Johnny over the years, as an actor he had separated himself from the character. He had moved on: "I've lived with *The Karate Kid* for three-plus decades, and Johnny Lawrence has always been in my periphery," Zabka says. "I've always had an affinity for him, I've always felt like

there was more to the character, but I'd let him go and was happy where he was memorialized in pop culture." Then, in September 2016, came an unexpected email from Heald, asking if they could meet to discuss a project. "I'd met Jon and Hayden when Josh and I were filming *Hot Tub Time Machine*, and I liked their work. I liked their sensibilities and their humor, so when Josh said he had a project to discuss, I was super excited. I came into the meeting with ears wide open and heart wide open."

The four guys met to discuss the potential series over a meal at a Mexican restaurant. "As the waiters were trying to deliver chips, the guys shooed them away, and then they came at me like a three-headed dragon," Zabka says. "They had the most perfectly polished pitch I've ever heard, and each of them took turns spit-firing *Cobra Kai* to me, pretty much as we know it today."

Zabka was overwhelmed but excited, if a bit cautious. First, he wanted to be sure the show would retain the heart of *The Karate Kid*, which was, after all, a family film. (The *Harold & Kumar* films and *Hot Tub Time Machine* were both R-rated and contained more adult humor.) Next was the question of Johnny— sure, he would be more three-dimensional, but would he still be the asshole? Zabka needed some reassurance that he wouldn't be. "Johnny was known as the villain of *The Karate Kid*, and I didn't want to repeat that," Zabka says. "I didn't want this to end with him getting the proverbial crane kick to the face, and have him carry the torch of the ultimate douche of all time." The guys confirmed that this version of Johnny Lawrence would have heart, and Zabka walked away convinced that they had tapped into the core of Johnny that he had seen all along. "I almost texted them, and for posterity I wish I had, but I remember saying, 'The Johnny Lawrence in me has opened one crusty eye and I feel like I see Ali standing over me.'"

The group now had to sell Ralph Macchio, who they knew would be more resistant to revisiting his old role. "Ralph is extremely protective of Daniel LaRusso, and extremely protective of the legacy of that franchise," Heald says. "He'd been on record for many years saying he had no interest in ever putting on the gi and the headband and playing that character again because he felt like the story was left on the field." Still, they asked Macchio's reps if they could fly to New York for a meeting. "We hoped he would appreciate that we were coming at this from a little bit of a richer storytelling perspective and not just trying to say, 'It's *The Karate Kid,* but it's now.'"

The guys were right about one thing: Macchio was resistant to opening the Daniel LaRusso vault. "For thirty-something years, I said no to everyone who had an idea of how to bring Daniel LaRusso into the present day or do a sequel," Macchio says. "No one ever came to me with a great idea. It was always some version of, 'You're an old guy now, and you have a problem.' Also, Pat Morita [who played Mr. Miyagi] had passed away in 2005, and that partnership was paramount, in my eyes, to what *The Karate Kid* was and the success of it—those father-son elements and mentor-student elements, all those themes that are ingrained into the movies. I had no desire to fly solo." Macchio also believed that the legacy of *The Karate Kid* was growing on the internet, with new fan theories and within fan communities, and he wasn't sure he wanted to mess with that. "I always felt that the movie was bigger—certainly bigger than the actor in it—and there are some things you just don't want to touch again. It was so precious to me, I wanted to leave it be, rather than say 'Okay, let's dig up these characters again and find a new angle.'"

Still, as newer forms of storytelling became popular, Macchio admits he wondered if there could be an approach that would work. In 2010, he did a four-minute *Funny or Die* video called "Wax On, Fuck Off," a parody trailer for a fake documentary in which he tries to become a Hollywood bad boy. "It was the greatest ever, but other than that spoof, it was more comfortable to let the legacy stand than risk tainting what it had become," Macchio says.

But in Hollywood, timing is everything, and the call telling him that Heald, Hurwitz, and Schlossberg had an idea came at the perfect moment. *Creed,* the Michael B. Jordan movie that picked up with Apollo Creed's son Adonis, had recently come out, which provided a model for offering a fresh take on an already-established universe without creating another sequel. Macchio had taken note. Instead of saying no right away, he agreed to hear the guys out. Of that first interaction, Macchio says: "They are the three biggest *Karate Kid* fans you will ever find—it was palpable how much they loved the movie." The meeting in New York started with a discussion of themes like bullying, and fathers and sons. "William and I always joke that we wish we had a videotape of

what he was pitched versus what I was pitched, because they certainly led off our meeting with all the things they knew I would want to hear."

Those things included Daniel LaRusso's happy marriage and successful business, and the enduring legacy of Mr. Miyagi. Given that the show would be something of a redemption story for Johnny, Macchio wanted to be sure Daniel, as his foil, wasn't a straight villain. He also, of course, wanted to honor the central relationship of the films. "I could only entertain the next step if I truly believed that the essence and the spirit of Miyagi would be woven throughout, whether in Daniel's lesson to his kids, or when Daniel himself is going through a midlife crisis. I didn't want to lose those elements, because they are the heart and soul of who that character was, and why we rooted for and loved this kid." That *Cobra Kai* would retain those elements was something Heald, Hurwitz, and Schlossberg assured him from the get-go.

One thing they didn't reveal right away? The show's name. "When they finally dropped that the title would be *Cobra Kai*, I remember that feeling like, 'Wait, if this thing works, I'm going to be in a show called *Cobra Kai*?'" Macchio jokes. "It's like Luke Skywalker being in a show called *Darth Vader*." Still, the screenwriters' approach was convincing enough that Macchio could stomach the new title, and he signed on.

ROBERT MARK KAMEN

CREATOR OF *THE KARATE KID* FRANCHISE

The guys called me up and told me about the series, then visited me for a weekend and we talked about their ideas. I laughed all weekend because I couldn't believe these guys: They have mined all three films I wrote and stolen whatever they could, and turned it into something quite amazing. I say it to them all the time: "You're absolutely shameless." They admit it. They laugh and say, "We know, and by the way, are there any other things we should know? Any secret techniques?"

I have been doing Okinawan Goju karate since I was seventeen and now I'm seventy-four. I've had the good fortune of having great teachers who were very close to the Okinawan source of it, so I know a million billion things that can be turned into the a-ha *Karate Kid* moments, like "Wax on, wax off." It comes from a deep understanding of the art of Okinawan Goju which we call Miyagi-Do, but is really an Okinawan karate system. So I know a lot about it, like the pressure points technique. I haven't told them everything—I've kept lots of stuff to myself.

But they are great for calling me up and telling me what they are doing. They are just wonderful people, which can be rare in this business. I love the whole thing—how smart, how good, how organic, how funny. So much of it is so funny. For me, this is a karate teenage soap opera set in the Valley. That's what it is, and my interest in it is how they have expanded the universe to have all these different story lines going—there's an adult story line, a teenage story line, love interests, rivalries. They've been so smart and so relevant.

It will be interesting to see how the Miyagi-verse expands and permeates the culture even more than it already has. *Cobra Kai* has really permeated the culture, the way *The Karate Kid* did when it first came out. It has extended beyond just being a television show.

I love the Easter eggs they hide. There was a scene I wrote in *Karate Kid II* because we needed a heroic moment for Daniel, so I made up this typhoon where Daniel saves a little girl who is on a lookout nest or a telephone pole. I thought nothing of it. And then I'm watching season three and there is the girl [Yuna, played by Traci

Toguchi] who is the head of Doyona International and she is throwing Ralph the lifeline, "Once you saved me, Daniel-san, and now I'm saving you," and she makes sure that he can still represent the cars. And I called the guys up and was like "What is wrong with you people? How do you remember this stuff!?" They remember stuff in the movies that I never even think about, and they make Easter eggs out of them. Some of the stuff they do is hysterical. I love it!

My daughter refuses to watch *Cobra Kai* because she's sick of me and *The Karate Kid*, but all her friends watch it. I said to the guys, when you have the new girl why don't you name her 'Tory with a Y' like 'Ali with an I,' who is my oldest daughter. And I didn't tell my youngest daughter I was doing this and then her phone started blowing up.

You'll also see in season four, the opening sequence, when Terry Silver kicks a wine bottle in half—that is Kamen Wines. I have a very successful wine brand off my vineyard, and they used my wine. No one would notice it but it was a lot of fun.

With the headliners in place—both as lead actors and executive producers—and all the necessary permissions granted, the next step was to find *Cobra Kai* a platform. The writers thought the show might land with Hulu, Netflix, or HBO, but decided to start the pitch process with executives at YouTube, in what they then considered a practice round. "We looked at YouTube as a place for six-minute viral cat videos or funny clips of someone

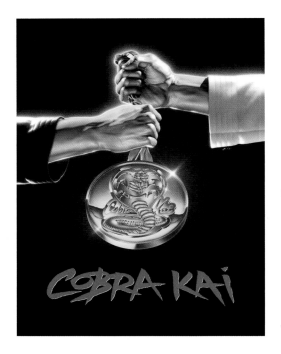

falling down," Heald says. "There was a little bit of scripted content that was richer, but we didn't know who was watching it and we didn't know a lot about the platform itself. So, we viewed that first pitch as a chance to go in and work out the kinks before we pitched the other streamers around town."

Macchio, Zabka, Heald, Hurwitz, and Schlossberg met with Susanne Daniels, head of what was then called YouTube Red, YouTube's paid ad-free offering that was looking to launch original scripted programming. As the team was nearing the end of its pitch, Daniels turned the tables and began to pitch the *Cobra Kai* guys on YouTube Red, selling it as the perfect home for their show. "YouTube said, 'We want this show, we want it to be what *House of Cards* was to Netflix in their early days. We will give you our full support and put this show first and foremost among our content,'" Heald recalls. "It was exactly what we needed: to be given the complete creative freedom to make the series we wanted to make."

YouTube wanted *Cobra Kai* quickly, so in less than two months the team had to be in Atlanta to shoot the first season. The guys immediately got to work—casting the characters, building the writers' room, hiring a cinematographer. Suddenly, the project they'd been thinking about, in some form or another, for more than a decade was really happening.

COMPOSERS
ZACH ROBINSON AND LEO BIRENBERG

In our very first meeting for *Cobra Kai*, Jon Hurwitz looked directly into our eyes and with complete and utter earnestness said, "You don't understand, *The Karate Kid* is our *Star Wars*." Ever since that moment, we've approached the score for *Cobra Kai* with Jon's words in mind. Yes, the story takes place within the confines of the San Fernando Valley, but its scope rivals even the most celebrated of Hollywood epics. Our job as composers is to relay information that the audience may not get by simply watching the screen. It is by listening that the audience is able to understand the weight of the story. In a sense, the score gives the viewer permission to buy into the fantastical world in which *Cobra Kai* takes place. We often joke about how there is no limit to how big the score can get; it is a rare occurrence for the creators to ask us to pull it back or tone it down to say, "Guys, you might want to pull it back here." The only way to score this show is to go all in.

Our score always comes from a place of sincerity and respect for the source material. When you hear a 1980s-style training montage in the show, it comes from a place of true admiration and reverence, not mockery.

Through fifty episodes, we've developed themes for not only the majority of characters, but also for dojos, rivalries, locations, and memories. Most of our cues feature multiple motifs used to summon previous moments in the series. We've also created quite the musical playground utilizing different sound palettes, ranging from hair metal to cinematic orchestra to retro-inspired synthwave, all of which contribute to our unique *Cobra Kai* soundscape. The fun, of course, comes from mixing and matching these themes and palettes. When Daniel starts to train alongside Eagle Fang in season four, for example, we hear his melodies played by an electric guitar, an instrument normally tied to Johnny Lawrence.

It takes a village to bring this massive score to life, and we work with an unbelievably talented crew of musicians as well as a superb orchestrator, music editor, and score mixer. Every episode features an eighty-piece orchestra recorded in Budapest as well as layers of guitar, bass, and drums recorded in Los Angeles.

It is an amazing honor to be a part of the *Karate Kid* legacy, and we are forever grateful to Jon, Josh, Hayden, and, of course, the incredible fan base for trusting us with such a beloved story.

One of the most thrilling moments, Heald recalls, was seeing Macchio and Zabka in front of the camera together. "It was exciting just to be in building lobbies for pitch meetings with them," he says. "I mean, we were inhabiting the same space as the Karate Kid and Johnny Lawrence. Then, showing up on set and seeing them act together as these characters for the first time in thirty-three years? That was special. And that feeling and those butterflies continued throughout that whole first season. There were days and moments where Jon, Hayden, and I would look at each other and it was like, 'Look at that! That's the bad guy from *The Karate Kid* right there!' We couldn't shake that feeling."

Cobra Kai premiered on May 2, 2018, on YouTube Red, still a relatively new streaming platform when it came to original content. "The day it came out, it felt like validation of everything we believed, in terms of this being a franchise that mattered to people," Schlossberg says. "There was a huge influx of viewers to the first two episodes. The reaction from both critics and the online audience was so positive. It opened in as amazing a way as we could have hoped."

Still, the show wasn't exactly a household name, because the YouTube Red audience was small when compared to its titanic peers. "It felt awesome on YouTube, it was exciting, and anyone who had actually seen the show loved it," Hurwitz says. "But you did feel underneath the surface that most people hadn't seen it, because they couldn't access it. It always felt like 'if only we could get more eyeballs on it . . .'"

Season two premiered a year later, also to critical acclaim, after which the team shot a third season. But before that season was released, what is now called YouTube Premium decided to stop producing scripted original programming, leaving the show stranded. So, in 2020, with season three in the can, the *Cobra Kai* creators went back to the market in hopes of selling the show to a new platform. "We felt very confident that someone would want it, and eventually the ideal place, Netflix, stepped up," Schlossberg says. The streaming platform released the first two seasons of *Cobra Kai* on August 28, 2020, leaving the show intact, shot for shot. If the show was small but mighty on YouTube, it was an overnight sensation on Netflix. It debuted at number one on the Netflix series chart and, within a month, had been streamed by fifty million member accounts.

The impressive numbers were due in part, the showrunners surmise, to

the fact that *Cobra Kai* appeals to fans of a wide range of viewing categories: sports drama, action, comedy, YA teen romance, and, naturally, those who had previously watched *The Karate Kid*. "Once it was in the on-platform advertising and being served to those who *might* be interested, it took on a life of its own," Hurwitz says. "Netflix viewers noticed *Cobra Kai* and gave it a shot, and one thing we hear over and over is that when you start watching this show, you don't stop. So people were bingeing it, and once the algorithm sees that, they feed it to more people."

Almost instantaneously, *Cobra Kai* was infecting fans everywhere. "All of a sudden, the success we'd enjoyed at YouTube Red felt like we'd been swimming in a pond and now we were in this ocean, because it was on an international level," Hurwitz says. "Whoopi Goldberg was talking about it on *The View* and the Pioneer Woman was talking about it on the Food Network and I was like, 'What the hell is going on here?' It was everything we'd hoped for."

With five seasons now under its belt, and a rabid fan base of Miyagi-Do, Cobra Kai, and Eagle Fang devotees, *Cobra Kai* shows no signs of slowing down. "I always knew it was going to be as big as it is right now, but it's not as big now as I think it's going to be in a couple of years," Heald says. "We are finally experiencing the show living where it belongs, with the audience who wants to see it—the adults who loved *The Karate Kid* in their childhoods, and the kids and teens who are discovering this world for the first time. The fan base is enormous and hungry, and it makes us buckle down and go faster and think more outside the box in terms of these characters and stories and the entire Miyagi-verse. It's exciting to think of what it could be, and what it should be. It hasn't even hit its peak."

COBR
NEVE

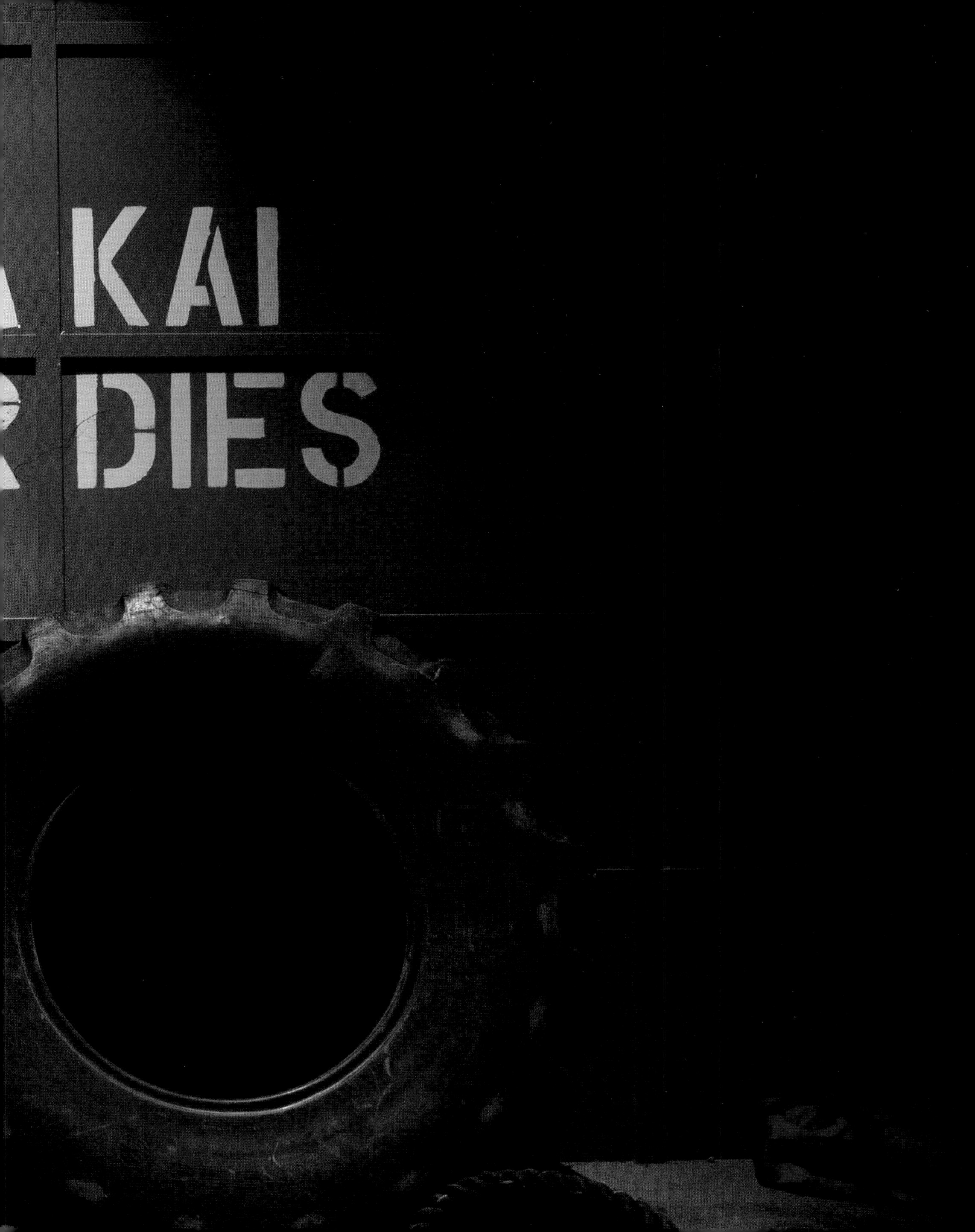
KAI
DIES

01
COBRA KAI

"FEAR DOES NOT EXIST IN THIS DOJO"

Strike First. Strike Hard. No Mercy.

If Johnny Lawrence internalized any lessons as a kid, these three rules—the mantras of the Cobra Kai dojo—were it. Always play offense. Hit your enemy before they hit you. And never, ever show weakness.

While teenage Johnny was taught never to back down from a fight, the man playing him always believed there was more to the character than the *Karate Kid* movies let on. "For me to step into the skin of a teenage Johnny Lawrence, I had to find his goodness, I had to find his heart," actor William Zabka says. "I found that at the very end of the *Karate Kid* script, when Johnny hands Daniel the trophy, and says, 'You're all right, LaRusso.' And also, when Kreese tells him to sweep the leg, but Johnny doesn't want to. He was a well-intentioned kid with wrong teaching."

Still, when viewers first glimpse Johnny in the pilot episode of *Cobra Kai*, not much has changed. In fact, he's right where viewers left him at the end of *The Karate Kid*—facedown and passed out, though this time in bed at his crappy apartment rather than on a karate mat. Three decades after the fateful All Valley tournament, Johnny's circumstances are different than they once were—gone are the Encino mansion and the motorcycle and the wingmen by his side. There's some early evidence of his humanity, most notably in a soccer photograph of his young son taped to his refrigerator, but he's in many ways still a bully, and he's unquestionably still stuck in the '80s. "The idea that we really grew to love, early in the writing process, was Johnny as this guy who peaked in high school, and the best time of his life was 1984, when he was 17 and a karate champion," Josh Heald says. "It naturally brings with it a generational comedy, where he doesn't really relate not only to present society but woke society. He can't understand teenagers or millennials."

The Johnny Lawrence of 2018, the year the show premiered on YouTube Red, is a beer-loving part-time handyman living in an apartment complex in

JOHNNY LAWRENCE

DOJO: Eagle Fang, Cobra Kai (former)

ALLIES: Daniel LaRusso (sometimes), John Kreese (former)

NEMESES: Daniel LaRusso (sometimes), John Kreese

CHARACTER PHILOSOPHY: "It doesn't matter if you're a loser, a nerd, or a freak. All that matters is that you become badass."

LOVE INTERESTS: Carmen Diaz (girlfriend), Ali Mills (former), Shannon Keene (former)

FAMILY: Robby Keene (son), Sid Weinberg (stepfather)

Reseda, the same neighborhood where his rival Daniel LaRusso lived as a teenager three decades before. He drives a Pontiac Firebird, watches the *Iron Eagle* and *Rambo* movies over breakfasts of Coors Banquet and fried bologna, and, after sabotaging most of his relationships—through a combination of drinking, bad decisions, and mistrust of other people—is mostly a loner. When Miguel Diaz, a teenager who just moved in across the hall, introduces himself, Johnny utters his very first line of the series: "Great, more immigrants."

It's the kind of tone-deaf comment that gives the audience a clear glimpse into who Johnny is at the start of the series: bitter, distrusting, generally uninterested in other people, and completely dismissive of any efforts to be woke. (A word he surely doesn't even know.) This is, after all, a guy who eventually tells his students to "Leave your asthma and your peanut allergies and all that other made-up bullshit outside," and that "Babes love it when you treat them like crap." But Zabka admits he wasn't so keen on the extent of Johnny's initial bad attitude at first. "Josh, Jon, and Hayden really just beat him down to a pulp," he says.

Still, Heald, Hurwitz, and Schlossberg were committed to their vision. "We really believed people want to see Johnny be an asshole," Hurwitz says. "That's part of why they show up, to see the character as they remember him. But now they want to understand that asshole. They want to root for that asshole, and maybe watch him become less of an asshole over time."

In his first redeeming moment of the pilot, Johnny's motivations remain largely selfish. When he sees Miguel getting beat up in the parking lot of his go-to strip mall, Johnny, who's sitting nearby eating a slice of pizza, intervenes—but only after Miguel gets hit so hard he knocks into Johnny's prized Firebird. "Johnny's okay with this kid getting the crap beat out of him as long as it's ten feet away," Heald says. "But the second the fight bumps into his twenty-year-old car, now he's involved." It's a moment that tells the audience everything they need to know about modern-day Johnny: he may notice bullies, but he's not going to go out of his way to stop them.

When he does step in, his retort is, "Leave the dork alone." Thirty years may have passed, but Johnny still relates to the bullies. "We wanted to set up

series, and we felt like there was something fun about him staying true to the persona that most people knew him for," Schlossberg says.

Although Johnny fights the high school bullies in that first episode for largely selfish reasons, the battle initiates a relationship that's at the heart of *Cobra Kai*. Watching his enemies get their asses kicked spurs Miguel to beg Johnny for help in the form of karate lessons. "Forget it, I don't do karate anymore," Johnny tells him.

It might seem like an unlikely beginning to an epic mentorship, but it's not without precedent. "What people remember about Mr. Miyagi is the wisdom and the affection and the friendship that builds between him and Daniel, but if you look at him at the very beginning of *The Karate Kid*, he's not eager to meet Daniel LaRusso. He's not excited about this new kid in the building," Hurwitz says. "He sees him as more of a nuisance, just as Johnny sees Miguel in *Cobra Kai*."

Another echo of the Miyagi-Daniel relationship in Johnny and Miguel's connection is the culture clash that exists between them. Johnny's a white guy who grew up rich, while Miguel comes from an Ecuadorian family that has struggled to get by. He's raised by a single mother who came to America to escape a dangerous husband, and they live with his wisecracking Spanish-

Johnny's Training Ideas

- Kick a hornet's nest (bonus points for a headbutt).
- Stand in the middle of the highway during rush hour. Don't flinch.
- Swim through giant lobster tank? Check with aquarium.
- Put kids in a well, make them climb out. Will need a well.
- Make them fight on a roller coaster (need access to carnival rides—ask Cutter).
- Fight fire with fire—teach them to punch through flaming bricks (note to self—disable smoke alarm first).
- Make them walk through a carwash and dodge those scrubby things.
- Paintball, but with none of that body armor bullshit. And the kids don't get guns either. I just shoot at them.

speaking grandmother. "In the very first days of planning the show, we were considering who would be the right student to learn from Johnny Lawrence and his methods," Hurwitz says. "We liked the idea of the two of them coming from two very different backgrounds and cultures. Not just because of Mr. Miyagi and Daniel, but because there's something special about the universality of mentorship. People can be different from you, and you can still form these very close bonds."

Over the course of the series, Johnny and Miguel find support, solace, and encouragement in each another. And while mentorships of all ages and types are built over the course of the *Cobra Kai* seasons, the Johnny-Miguel relationship is the one that kick-started it all. "Johnny helps Miguel adjust to a new town and stand up to bullies, because he's a kid who could use a little bit of fight in him. But in a lot of ways, Miguel becomes a mentor to Johnny as well, opening his eyes to the ways of the modern world," Hurwitz points out.

In addition to schooling Johnny in the dos and don'ts of DMs and Facebook likes ("Shorter messages are way cooler. Like, this [message] just looks desperate. And a little creepy. Sending her this would be like if you liked all her photos . . . oh, no"), Miguel fills another void in Johnny's life: the one left by his son, Robby, who Johnny has failed for the last sixteen years. "I think Johnny looks at Miguel as a chance to do right with a kid, because with Robby, he made some big mistakes," says Xolo Maridueña, who plays Miguel. "And Miguel

---

JOHNNY: **"Are you sure you're ready? Because once you go down this path there's no turning back."**

MIGUEL: **"You're going to be my karate teacher?"**

JOHNNY: **"No. I'm going to be your sensei."**

---

looks at Johnny as something of a father figure, because that role has been missing in his life. They truly need each other."

The pain of Johnny's failure with Robby reverberates through much of *Cobra Kai*. The viewer sees it in Johnny's eyes when his son gets injured in the season one All Valley Tournament, or in Johnny's reaction to a teenage Robby connecting with his various rivals. But the viewer also sees how Johnny's

bond with Miguel gives him purpose, even if it's expressed in crude, often misdirected, and very *Johnny-esque* ways. "That Johnny didn't even have the guts to walk across the street and see his son's face when Robby was born, that is a deep wound that he can never make right," Zabka says. "But in lieu of that relationship, to meet this kid who lives across the hall and suddenly looks at him like he's the greatest thing since sliced bread? He's finally got someone on whom he can use all those paternal skills and love, as skewed as they are. One of my favorite scenes in the first season is when Johnny goes to [Miguel's mom] Carmen's door and says, 'He's the only kid that's never given up on me. He's the only *person* that's never given up on me.' You've got this kid who finally needs Johnny, which gives him a purpose. So he stands up for him, and ultimately ends up becoming his sensei."

The final scene of the pilot episode establishes the relationship between Johnny and Miguel that will help revive the Cobra Kai dojo, and it includes a conversation that changes the course of both of their lives, and indeed the show:

> JOHNNY: "Are you sure you're ready? Because once you go down this path there's no turning back."
>
> MIGUEL: "You're going to be my karate teacher?"
>
> JOHNNY: "No. I'm going to be your sensei. I'm going to teach you the style of karate that was taught to me. A method of fighting your pussy generation desperately needs. I'm not just going to teach you how to conquer your fears. I'm going to teach you how to awaken the snake within you. And once you do that, you'll be the one who's feared. You'll build strength. You'll learn discipline. And when the time is right . . . you'll strike back."

Zabka definitely had some questions when he was first pitched the idea that Johnny would rebuild Cobra Kai. "This is the snake that bit him, so I couldn't understand why he was opening Pandora's box. Why doesn't he open Johnny Lawrence Karate?" Zabka says. "But as far as the dojo goes, there's an empowering feeling for Johnny, because those were his glory days. This is the place where he thrived. And there's also a bit of him trying to undo what went

wrong—he's facing his demons. As much as it really is Pandora's box, he's trying to better himself."

Deciding what the new iteration of Cobra Kai would look like was an exciting exercise for the show's creators. "When you ask yourself what kind of dojo Johnny is going to build—well, he's going to model it after what he knows," Heald says. He takes a check from his stepfather, Hollywood producer Sid Weinberg (played by late legendary actor Ed Asner), and puts down a deposit on a space in the very same strip mall where he witnessed Miguel's bullying only days earlier. He stencils six words in black paint on the white wall: *Strike First. Strike Hard. No Mercy.* They're the same words he was compelled to recite during his young Cobra Kai days. "For Johnny, it doesn't make sense to do karate in the backyard like Miyagi. Given his finances, and the fact that he had only one student, it would've been more reasonable for him to say to Miguel, 'Great, let's go out in the courtyard and I'll teach you a few things.' But no. For Cobra Kai, you have to have a strip mall location, it has to have an office that looks out on the dojo. That comes with the gi to some degree," Heald says. "When he builds the dojo, Johnny is still naïve to the fact that there is poison in the Cobra Kai waters as opposed to just poison in the teacher himself. The dojo he creates speaks to the question of 'What does Johnny think Cobra Kai is?' It's an important question that takes some time to unravel."

At the end of episode one, when Johnny finally puts on the infamous black headband, he's still an underdog. He's just lost his job, his Firebird is in the shop (after getting hit by a car driven by Yasmine, a friend of Daniel LaRusso's daughter, Samantha), and he hasn't seen his son in years. And this all comes to light against the backdrop of Daniel LaRusso, who—judging by the number of billboards and car commercials he stars in across the city—has a good reputation and financial success.

Johnny's not the only one sitting at the bottom of the social totem pole. Miguel and the other eventual Cobra Kai students are also struggling, constantly mocked or picked on for being weak or timid or nerdy. When creating the physical Cobra Kai space, the creators wanted to echo that underdog mentality. It's hard to tell in the shots that ultimately made the pilot, but the Cobra Kai storefront was intentionally designed to indicate that it was

most recently a ballet studio. "That's the reason why there's a big mirror, and you can see evidence of an old ballet bar on the wall," Heald says. "We wanted to show that it had been a space that hosted a similar business in the past and failed. So right out of the gate, Johnny's renting a place that could not support a different kind of studio, but he still feels like, 'If I put on the headband and I get that kid in here, that's all it takes.'"

It's a bumpy start for Johnny—he has trouble attracting students, his space needs urgent repairs, he has to sublet the studio to a yoga class to make rent—but after a fight in which Miguel uses his new karate moves on Kyler and the other bullies in the school cafeteria, Cobra Kai is overrun with students. And, like his sensei before him, Johnny doesn't go easy on them. "When I look around this dojo, I don't see Cobra Kai material," he tells his first full class. "I see losers, I see nerds, I see a fat kid with a funny hat with tits popping out." It's classic Johnny Lawrence—he's trying to inspire greatness in these kids, but the only way he knows how to do that is by hurling insults at them.

While the Johnny character is brash and offensive, actor William Zabka is anything but. Behind the scenes, Maridueña says listening to Zabka berate the young actors was both jarring and hilarious. "William is such a wonderful

castmate to play opposite of, and he's truly the nicest person I've ever met. It's funny to see him saying all of these crude, ridiculous things on camera, because the second we wrap he's like 'I'm so sorry, I had to say that.' He's the sweetest man ever."

The comedy of that juxtaposition—the good guy spewing nasty insults—translates on screen. "These kids are all a big experiment for Johnny, and it shows to hilarious effect," Zabka says. "He's wielding a big sword but he doesn't quite know how to use it or what exactly it does. So he's making a lot of mistakes with these kids and pointing them in some wrong directions and telling them to punch each other in the face."

In spite of all that, Johnny builds a loyal following: first Miguel, then Aisha Robinson—Miguel's friend who is also being bullied, and the first female fighter to be introduced into the *Cobra Kai* world—and eventually the rest of the Cobra Kai students. "It's a tough-love way of teaching lessons," Maridueña says. "But it starts working once Miguel is like, 'Oh, okay, this is just how this guy is. I'm going to have to accept it for what it is and learn something.'"

It helps, of course, that his students get an early glimpse of what Zabka calls Johnny's "heart of a lion." Just after his biting assessment of the "losers and nerds," Johnny gives a shout-out to his first two success stories. "In my

Miguel's Topics to Cover With Sensei

- Music didn't stop in the early '90s.
- Electric cars (he won't like this).
- Does Sensei know the Cold War ended? Double-check.
- Toxic masculinity and why it's bad (baby steps with this one).
- Nerds are all rich now (see Gates, Zuckerberg, Musk).
- Acceptable terms for women (NOT babes and chicks).
- Movies without training montages.

short time as a sensei, I've also seen some miracles," he says, with a glance toward Miguel and Aisha. "So maybe there's some hope for you yet."

One of his most loyal devotees—and an early fan favorite—emerges in an unexpected student. Eli Moskowitz is a severely bullied high school kid who was born with a cleft lip, the surgery for which has left a noticeable scar. For the first half of *Cobra Kai*'s initial season, Eli barely speaks, but after seeing Miguel stand up to the bullies in the lunchroom, he joins the legions of students eager to learn the Cobra Kai ways. Perhaps unsurprisingly, Johnny doesn't go easy on Eli. He calls him "lip," and asks if he's "one of those challenged kids." In one particularly brutal exchange, Johnny tells Eli he can't stop calling out the scar because it's too hard to look away. "If you want to be something other than a nerd with a scar on his lip, then you gotta flip the script, okay? Get a face tattoo or gouge your eye out. We'll call you patch, all right? No, don't do that, you'll still look like a freak." Eli storms out, seemingly tortured by Johnny's harsh words, but when he shows up to the next class, he's sporting a giant blue mohawk.

"I flipped the script," Hawk, formerly known as Eli, says in response to Johnny and his fellow students' dropped jaws. It's another indication that Johnny's methods, unorthodox as they are, might be working. And thus, one of *Cobra Kai*'s most pivotal fighters is born.

Jacob Bertrand, the actor who plays Hawk, says his character's loyalty to Johnny and Cobra Kai was first inspired by Miguel's fight in the lunchroom. "Watching Miguel stand up to the same kids who have been picking on Eli for years—and watching him beat them up in such a crazy fashion—it was as though the entity of Johnny became a god in his eyes," Bertrand says. "Eli is like, 'Holy shit, this man turned Miguel into a fricking superhero, and now he's standing up to the same guys I thought were unbeatable.'"

"I think viewers are finding themselves in these characters," Zabka says. "They're finding themselves in Hawk, who's been bullied and has been up against so much. And in Johnny, who's washed up and detached but trying to understand the world these kids are living in." Given Johnny's rough-around-the-edges approach, it would have been easy for not only his students to hate him, but for the audience to as well. Instead, this modern-day iteration of Johnny has become a true fan favorite, as have his dojos. Bertrand says he's heard similar support for the Cobra Kai dojo in unexpected places. "I was at prom, taking pictures, and my friend's dad came up to me—and this was back when we were still on YouTube Red—and he was like, 'Jacob, I just gotta say, all the guys at the fire station are with Cobra Kai.'"

It helps that today's television audience is more forgiving of an antihero than moviegoers in the '80s may have been. "A lot of the shows people love in this golden age of television, whether it's *Breaking Bad* or *Sopranos*, have these despicable characters that have other aspects of their humanity that you fall in love with," Schlossberg says. More modern shows, like *Succession, Killing Eve,* or even *Curb Your Enthusiasm*, similarly galvanize fans around a character (or characters) who, at least on the surface, seem unlikeable. The *Cobra Kai* creators were excited to give Johnny that same treatment.

Of course, as viewers originally learned in the *Karate Kid* films, when you have a bully for a teacher, it's easy to go astray. By the middle of season two, Hawk has arguably become worse than the guys who used to pick on him, and even Miguel is internalizing the concept of "no mercy," if only to prove something to his sensei. "Johnny is Miguel's point of contact into this world of karate, and he's the male figure Miguel has been yearning for his whole life. All he wants to do is make Johnny proud," Maridueña says. "He's willing to bend the rules a little bit and do some things that might be questionable, but it's all because he wants nothing more than to win a trophy. He wants to turn around and show it to Johnny and say, 'I did this for us.'"

Just as Johnny Lawrence earned the admiration and respect of his students on screen, Zabka became a sensei, too. "On camera he was saying some pretty terrible things to them, and trying to relate to them like a football coach in 1982, but off-camera there was this bond that still exists between all the actors who are or have been in the Cobra Kai dojo," Heald says. In fact, each year, on the last day of shooting, Zabka makes headbands commemorating the end of the season, and gives them to everyone on set, from background actors and camera assistants all the way up to the top-billed cast. "It's like a trophy that says, we went through something, we made it. It makes us feel like a family and it's wonderful to see that every year." (Zabka's not the only one. Wrap gifts have become a *Cobra Kai* tradition. One year, Ralph Macchio gave chopsticks to everyone on set; another year the creators gave out beach cruiser bikes. Since filming usually ends around Christmastime, Courtney Henggeler, who plays Amanda LaRusso, walks around with a Santa-sack-turned-grab-bag with presents like *Cobra Kai* coloring books and decks of cards.)

That *Cobra Kai* family grew to include a new cast member in the final moments of season one. Martin Kove, who plays villainous sensei John Kreese, first appears in the season one finale, as he steps through the doors of the Cobra Kai dojo. On-screen, Miguel has just won the All Valley Tournament, securing a victory over Robby in the finals after targeting his injured shoulder and taking the "no mercy" philosophy a little too seriously. At the same time, Johnny is starting to get clarity on his own karate philosophy—that perhaps being a badass isn't about picking on the weak, and maybe there's a place for mercy after all. It's in this moment, when he's beginning to realize he may need to forge his own karate path, that his old teacher enters the studio.

If Johnny Lawrence lives in the shades of gray between good guy and bad, Kreese is camped firmly in the dark side. He's the sensei who originated the way of the fist and who nearly beat up Johnny for losing to Daniel LaRusso back in the '80s. Johnny has plenty of pent-up rage when it comes to Kreese, but their relationship, like many on the show, is complicated. "Kreese is Johnny's blind spot. He was the father figure Johnny never had," Zabka says. "But when Kreese walks into the dojo at the beginning of season two and goes to shake Johnny's

THE ORIGINAL
COBRA KAI CREW:
WHERE ARE THEY NOW?

DUTCH: After a couple of arrests in the '90s and a trip to juvie, today the most aggressive of the original Cobra Kai gang is an inmate serving 10–20 years in Lompoc Federal Prison.

BOBBY BROWN: Now a pastor, Bobby preaches forgiveness, and he tries to help Johnny make amends, too. When Robby ends up in juvie and Miguel lands in the hospital, Bobby intervenes on behalf of both kids, getting his church to make a donation for Miguel's surgery, and taking a trip to visit Robby behind bars.

TOMMY: After battling an unnamed illness, Tommy died in the summer of 2018. But not before one final, epic trip with his oldest friends. Johnny, Bobby, and Jimmy visit Tommy in the hospital in *Cobra Kai* season two, and the foursome hop on their motorcycles for a day of drinking, playing pool, camping and, yes, a fight. Tommy dies in his sleep that night, after a heart-to-heart with Johnny under the stars.

JIMMY: Three decades after losing to Daniel LaRusso in the third round of the All Valley Tournament, Jimmy is married; he and his wife, Jenny, have two sons. Though it's been years since he's trained in karate, when he steps into the fight at the pool hall in *Cobra Kai* season two, he surprises himself by throwing a punch that shows he's still got it.

hand and Johnny slaps him and attacks him and they have this big fight? That's a lot of pain, a lot of anger, a lot of frustration."

Things remain tense until Johnny, suspicious of Kreese's stories from the years since losing the Cobra Kai dojo, discovers Kreese living in a veterans' shelter. Upon seeing his former sensei humbled and defeated, Johnny decides to give him a second chance. He lets Kreese back in to the dojo, allowing him to act as second in command, despite some of his students' reservations. "As irreverent and unorthodox as Johnny Lawrence is, he's still a fine teacher," says Kove. "John Kreese ultimately doesn't share that kind of compassion for students. For him, the purpose of Cobra Kai was to restructure weakness, and he believes that strength should always prevail. As he sees it, losing is a deterioration of the soul."

Kreese's blind devotion to his "no mercy" beliefs are what ultimately drive him and Johnny apart, but not before Kreese earns the loyalty of some of Johnny's most promising students. Hawk is the first to fall under his spell. "Eli never really had a super strong sense of self," Bertrand says. "Cobra Kai under Johnny becomes his identity. He suddenly has all this power—he can fight, girls are paying attention to him, he's popular. When Kreese comes in, this is the guy who taught his idol everything he knows, and now he's in the dojo telling stories of war and killing all these dudes. Half the stuff he says isn't even true but Kreese knows how to manipulate people and inspire loyalty in them, and Hawk is an easy target." Eventually, Hawk comes to his senses and rejects Kreese, but by that point the sensei has earned the loyalty of some other strong students: Tory, a female fighter with troubles at home, and Robby, who has lost trust in both his father and Daniel LaRusso, his former sensei.

Kreese's ability to manipulate comes in large part from his experiences as a soldier in Vietnam, a time in his life that viewers get to glimpse through flashbacks in season three. In one of the earliest flashbacks, Kreese, then a busboy, gets bullied by a diner patron who is played by Martin Kove's real-life son, Jesse Kove. Martin Kove says these glimpses into Kreese's backstory help crystallize how the character is able to command devotion from his karate recruits. "Most of these students suffered from bullying and losing their self-esteem. I think Kreese, as he would say, is creating soldiers who are tough

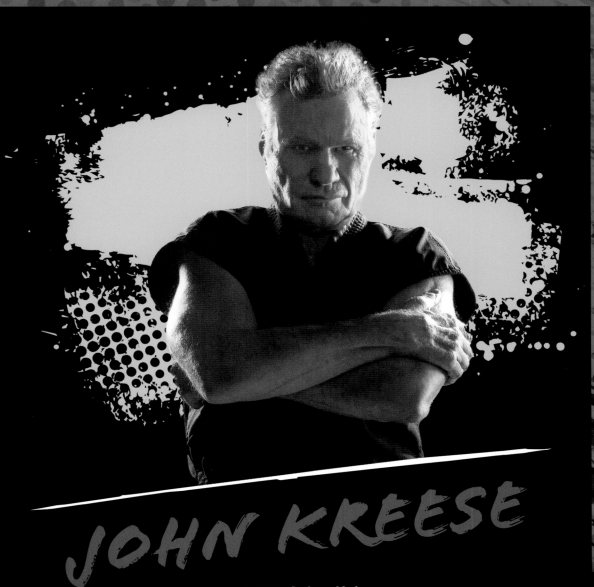

JOHN KREESE

DOJO: Cobra Kai

ALLIES: Terry Silver (sometimes), Tory Nichols

NEMESES: Daniel LaRusso, Johnny Lawrence (sometimes),

Amanda LaRusso, Nariyoshi Miyagi (former)

CHARACTER PHILOSOPHY: "Mercy is for the weak."

LOVE INTEREST: Betsy (former)

MARTIN KOVE (KREESE)

What has it been like to rejoin the Miyagi-verse and re-inhabit this epic character, after so long?

When I met with the writers prior to season one, Ralph and Billy were committed. I was mostly interested in not having the character be as one-dimensional as he was in *Karate Kid I, II,* and *III.* I had ideas of making him texturized with emotions and some vulnerable situations. At the time we met, I didn't know if they could write visions and dialogue as well as Robert Kamen, but I found they were actually light-years ahead of my expectations and had similar ideas about the character. Even though I wanted to come in on episode five, season one, they explained how imperative and dramatic it would be to arrive in episode ten, season one as a surprise character—a surprise, unwelcomed character.

What was it like to bring back Terry Silver and work with Thomas Ian Griffith again?

The event of bringing in another villain who was controversial and rocked the boat a little initially, as it was explained to me, was because the writers wanted ultimate redemption for my character. They told me their intention. That if we created a more villainous monster, then maybe only another hybrid villain such as John Kreese, who walks in both worlds, could challenge him and hopefully redeem himself in the future of the show.

What do you believe are John Kreese's ultimate values? What is driving him?

The values of John Kreese come from as far back as Vietnam and his experience there. He's been bullied in an arena far more dangerous than a karate tournament. Cobra Kai was created as an offensive sport, whereas Miyagi-Do's teachings of Mr. Miyagi focused on karate as a defensive art. Due to the experience of both Terry Silver and John Kreese in Vietnam, the purpose of Cobra Kai was to restructure weakness and moral discipline and focus on one's internal and external strength throughout life. Harsh as it may sound, this belief, this concept, this way of life has validity and will always have validity in our present world.

How was Kreese affected by his war experience, and how does that experience inform the man he still is all these years later?

John Kreese's life has been totally bittersweet. His father an alcoholic, his mother not well throughout his upbringing, which is why he has a sympathy and a camaraderie so easily established with our character Tory. John Kreese had very little support in his life emotionally, and unfortunately had to spend most spare hours working as an adolescent and as a teenager in the marketplace. Without family associations and support, John Kreese was on his own from the beginning. As a result, sensitivity was at a premium for this young man.

He trusted his superior officer, who had selfishly held back the news that John's one and only love, Betsy, had perished in a car crash. His war experience culminated with young Kreese surviving vicious hand-to-hand combat against this one-time idolized superior. It was a dark confrontation full of surprises and certainly violated the respect and love that our young hero had for his superior officer. Thus, his level of trust and belief in his fellow man had been minimized, culminating twenty years later with the disintegration of his relationship with his one-time fictional son, Johnny Lawrence.

How do Kreese's experiences inform how he teaches and relates to his students?
John Kreese only knows one way of instructing, and that is what he experienced in the war and what he has endured throughout his life, a lack of compassion and discipline from the majority of friends and enemies he has entertained over the last twenty years. Discipline and talent were the only things that have kept him alive to impart to his students. This man is not evil, but only caresses what he is familiar with.

Have you been surprised by the success and embrace of the show, all these years after the movies?
Every great movie or television show is based on the writing. We can coin "May the force be with you" from *Star Wars*, "Play it again, Sam" from *Casablanca*, or as far back as *Gone with the Wind* and Clark Gable saying, "Frankly, my dear, I don't give a damn." Great writing produces classic film situations. *Cobra Kai* is no different. The writing is superb and lends itself to people of all walks, all ages, all tastes to watch the show as a family. Like the old *Ed Sullivan Show*, there is something for everyone, and *Cobra Kai* and the writing is responsible for that. Our writers—Jon Hurwitz, Hayden Schlossberg, and Josh Heald—are wonderful at commanding the interests of the young audience who migrate to the show, because the younger characters on the show are gray and have similar problems to teenagers of today's society. The adults—Johnny Lawrence, Daniel LaRusso, and John Kreese—all share the problems of adulthood and coping with society and its demands. Adults who have seen the movies recommend them to the children, and the children—after watching *Cobra Kai*—recommend the series to their respective adults and their parents. This show has something for everyone. It's very meaningful. When you compare the villains and heroes from the movies to the characters in the series, personal identification for all fans is imminent. I'm proud to be part of something with the taste, creativity, and class of *Cobra Kai*.

and he's helping them to build armor. When they feel their inner strength and see the change they've gone through emotionally and physically, they can do nothing but celebrate Kreese's ideology," Kove says. "He's also loyal to his students, as long as they understand the concept of winning under any circumstances."

That "number one at all costs" approach leads Kreese to drive Johnny away and eventually take over Cobra Kai. "This is my dojo," he tells Johnny when he reveals he has claimed ownership of the property. "I founded Cobra Kai. It belongs to me. It always has, and it always will."

It's a blindside that sends Johnny reeling. "At first, Johnny felt like he could handle Kreese back in his life. He doesn't feel like the teenager under his thumb, and he even thinks he has some power over Kreese. But it's always been an abusive relationship," Zabka says. "Kreese is the core of Cobra Kai as we know it. He's the snake that bit Johnny, and he just can't help himself."

Creating Kreese's version of Cobra Kai meant building out a space more representative of the new sensei's outlook—more militant, less scrappy. "As Kreese takes over the dojo, the weapons on the wall and his military paraphernalia make more of an appearance," Hurwitz says, referencing the

swords and nunchucks that hang in the dojo in season three. "There's more emphasis on the back room with its darker elements." There's also an actual cobra in a cage. And as Cobra Kai evolves through seasons four and five, so too does the studio. When actor Thomas Ian Griffith returns as Terry Silver—the *Karate Kid Part III* villain and a former war buddy of Kreese—the dojo gets top-of-the-line exercise equipment and all-new designer workout gear

and warmup suits. Silver upgrades the dojo to a bigger space and takes over existing studios to open Cobra Kai franchises all over the city. A dojo, after all, is a product of its sensei.

After getting the boot from Cobra Kai, Johnny establishes his new dojo, Eagle Fang, so named because "There's only one animal that can kill a snake." But this time around there is no strip-mall storefront, no back office overlooking the studio. "It's been fun to write the development of Johnny's understanding of what makes a dojo," Hurwitz says. "He has his Eagle Fang students do karate in the park for a time, and that was sort of an experience where he said, 'You don't *need* a dojo to *be* a dojo.' And then in season four, we have this industrial

 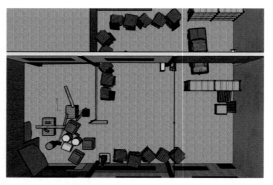

"There's only one animal that can kill a cobra. No, not a mongoose. A *real* animal. You want to rule the skies and kick major ass?

LEARN TO BITE LIKE
AN EAGLE."

space, which is really consistent with Eagle Fang Karate and the general danger and badassness of it—that rough-around-the edges mentality." For that space, the show's production designer took a portion of a giant warehouse and created what looks like an abandoned factory that Johnny repurposed into a dojo, turning old wooden planks or left-behind cinder blocks into exercise equipment. "It looks like Johnny's just squatting in this place," Hurwitz says. "It fits Johnny's spirit and his approach even more so than the original Cobra Kai dojo."

Eagle Fang's evolution is ongoing, as is its sensei's. "It's what I love about the character, and why I signed on to do this show," Zabka says. "Johnny is not going to be stuck, he's going to move forward. He's a work in progress. But his redemption story is not going to happen overnight. It's not going to happen in one or two seasons. And maybe he'll never really be redeemed—maybe what's broke is broke. But I sure hope not."

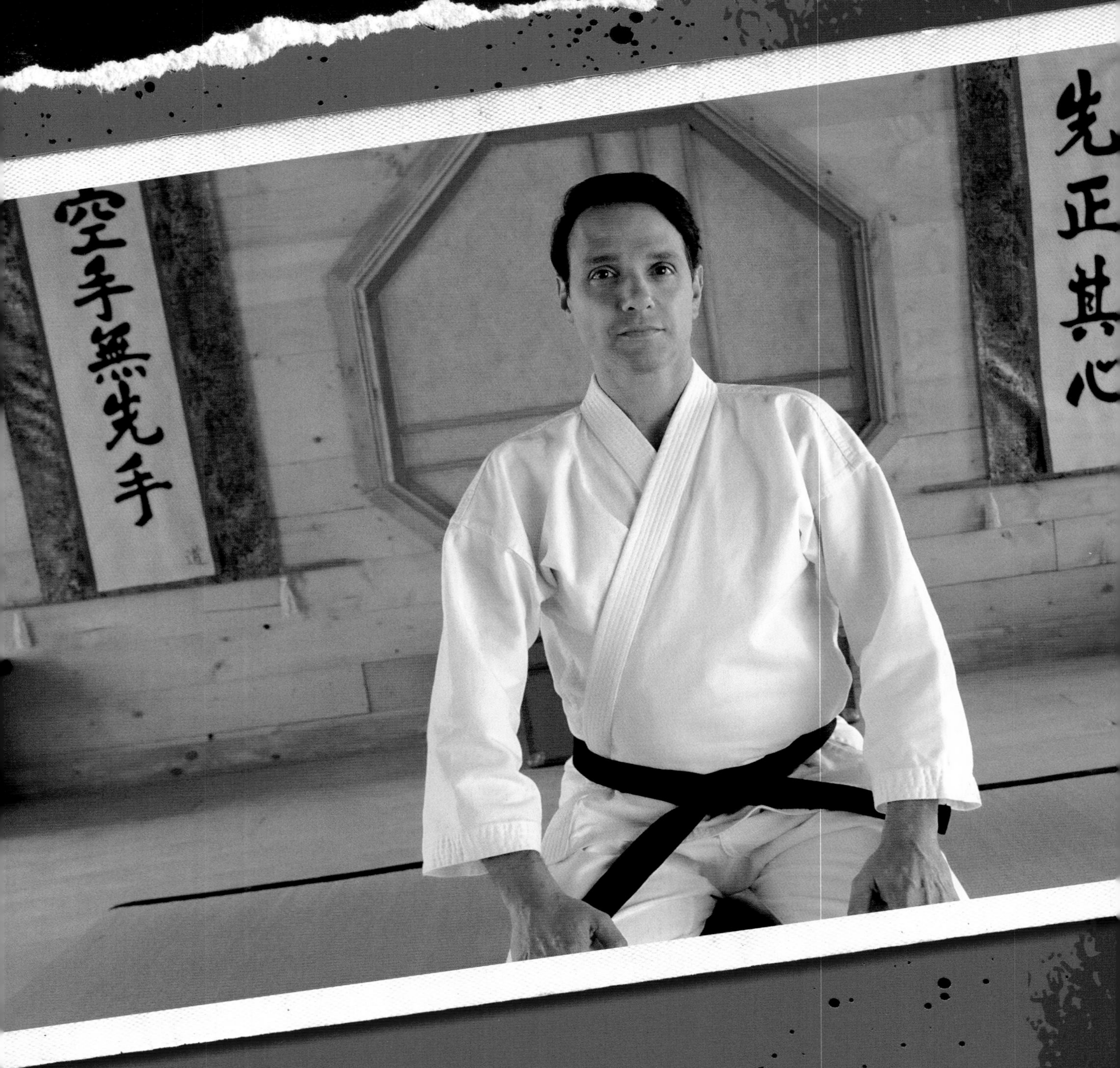
空手無先手
先正其心

02
MIYAGI-DO

"A MONUMENT TO BALANCE"

When stories are centered around rivalries, it's easy to peg one side as all good and the other as all bad. And given that *Cobra Kai* was conceived as a series with a major shift in perspective from its *Karate Kid* predecessors, Ralph Macchio knew it might be tempting for the creators to peg his character as the villain. "I wanted to be sure that we found our way to a balanced television series, where it's not just 'Okay, let's make Daniel the dick and Johnny the sympathetic character,'" Macchio says. "Sure, season one is clearly designed so that anytime Johnny was confronted with some form of Daniel LaRusso it was his worst nightmare, but I also wanted to honor the happily ever after that we left Daniel with in the movies." By the end of *The Karate Kid Part III,* Daniel has a second All Valley championship under his belt and has effectively put an end to the Cobra Kai dojo after it's revealed that its entrant fought dirty, and the dojo is banned from the tournament. The audience is left with an impression of Daniel as a young man of integrity, with a bright future ahead of him.

Staying true to the Daniel of the *Karate Kid* films was as critical to the showrunners as it was to Macchio. "It was really important to us to make sure the viewer sees what's going on in [Daniel's] house and sees that, this is not just somebody who took Mr. Miyagi's teachings and threw them in the trash, or used them for financial gain, and became a villain. It was important to show that everybody is trying to do right, but they each have their own perspectives and their own backstory."

Before viewers get any insight into Daniel's evolution over the last thirty years, they first see the same thing Johnny does: a giant LaRusso Auto Group billboard. On it is the image of Daniel LaRusso doing a karate kick next to the company slogan, "We kick the competition." When Johnny spots a LaRusso Auto Group TV commercial a few scenes later, the audience learns that the karate gimmick has been working for Daniel—he's "chopping prices" left and right and gifting customers with their very own bonsai tree as a sign of gratitude (for their business). It appears as if the martial art form he was taught as a kid—the one to be used "for defense only"—has now become a money-making tool, a stepping-stone on the ladder to financial success. In fact, the Daniel that Johnny (and the audience) sees in the commercial, with his perfectly tailored suits and well-groomed haircut, has a bit of a cheesy, maybe even slick, car salesman vibe. It doesn't appear to be what Mr. Miyagi had in mind when he taught Daniel about bonsai trees and crane kicks. In the series' second episode, the audience gets a firsthand look at Daniel's home life, where, by all visual signs, he appears to have made it. With Frank Sinatra crooning in the background of the opening montage, Daniel nearly floats through his day, waking up happily next to his beautiful wife, serving his two kids a hearty and healthy breakfast, and then dancing his way into work, where his employees light up at the sight of him. From an outsider's perspective, his personal and professional lives are in perfect balance.

But, as Daniel himself notes in the first season, things aren't always what they seem. While driving home at the end of that episode's "perfect day," Daniel

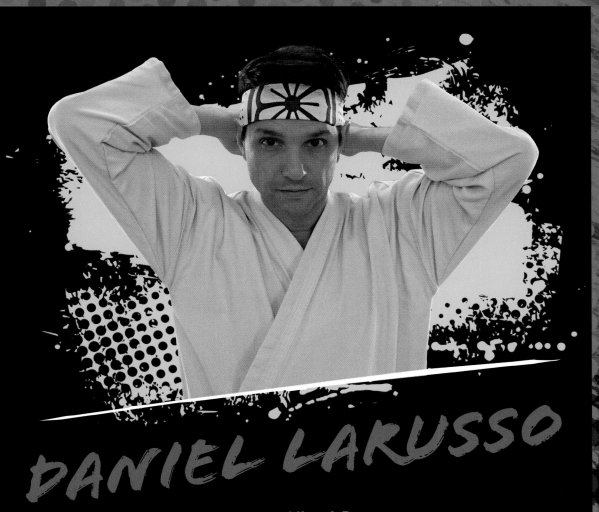

DANIEL LARUSSO

DOJO: Miyagi-Do

ALLIES: Johnny Lawrence (sometimes), Chozen Toguchi, Nariyoshi Miyagi (former)

NEMESES: Johnny Lawrence (sometimes), John Kreese, Terry Silver

CHARACTER PHILOSOPHY: "If you have hate in your heart, you have already lost."

LOVE INTERESTS: Amanda LaRusso (wife), Ali Mills (former), Kumiko (former)

FAMILY: Lucille LaRusso (mother), Samantha LaRusso (daughter), Anthony LaRusso (son), Louie LaRusso (cousin)

spots the Cobra Kai signage, now affixed above the strip mall storefront, and it becomes clear his life isn't so idyllic after all. The sign snaps him out of his dreamy haze, serving as a reminder of the demons of his past—facing off (not always successfully) against bullies, the evil influence of John Kreese, the loss of Mr. Miyagi, and just how far his life has strayed, for better and worse, from the Miyagi-Do student he once was. Through the remainder of the episode, Daniel's reality comes into focus: he's struggling to connect with his kids, who would rather play video games and host high school pool parties than spend time with their father, and he's worried that his success is turning his children into "privileged Encino brats," as he tells his wife, Amanda. Without Mr. Miyagi, who died in 2011, he's feeling lost and in need of guidance.

Adult Daniel LaRusso isn't entirely different from the teenage version, at least when it comes to seeking advice and a father figure. Macchio says he approached the role of adult Daniel with the same mindset he used to tackle the teenage version, despite the decades that had passed. "When I was playing the role back in 1983, it was just a heightened version of my own sensibilities, with a little bit more of a knee-jerk temper than I have personally. I'm a little bit more analytical, where LaRusso is immediately like '*What did you say?*' He acts first and only then steps back to sort of see what he's done, and that makes for better cinema than someone who figures things out first and doesn't make mistakes, which is what I try to do. So, when I returned to the role, I took that same model and added in the wisdom and experience of the last, at that point, thirty-four years." Like his character, Macchio has been married for decades and has a son and a daughter, though his real-life kids are in their twenties now. He could relate to where *Cobra Kai*'s Daniel was in life—professionally successful but also trying to juggle the pressures of career and family. "There were interesting parallels with Ralph and Daniel as adults," he says. "For the show, I just chose to amp up a little bit of the LaRusso East Coast essence— that 'act first, think later' impulse—just like I did decades prior. And it worked because it helped establish the conflict between him and Johnny, to have a piece of Daniel's teenage instincts still be part of who he is."

This time around, the rivalry has more nuance. "It's more of a level playing field," Zabka says. "We're meeting these guys where they are today, with all their baggage, so there's more humanity. There are layers of depth and character in Johnny and Daniel, who both have the best intentions, but also have their issues. And to watch them work it out, especially knowing their past, is comical but it's also human."

That mix of humanity and comedy is paramount. "When you are still talking about that rivalry and still living with it thirty-something years later, and you have all these open wounds that are so deep on both sides and you refuse to give an inch, it's naturally pretty hilarious," Josh Heald says. "The stakes of our universe are at once very serious and dramatic, and also very ridiculous and comedic."

And while the show adopts some self-awareness in tone, it's not a parody, and striking the balance between genuine emotion, drama, and humor is one of the most critical aspects of the series. The creators make it work by writing stories that are both heartfelt and high-stakes, and when things veer into the absurd, they let the characters themselves call it out. Amanda LaRusso might be the most vocal when it comes to flagging ridiculous moments. "She's an outsider to this universe, an outsider to the history, and she's able to look at it and say 'Wait a minute, you guys are karate rivals? And there's an older guy involved that you have issues with? Shouldn't you know better? Don't you have a family and a house and a career?'" Heald says. "She lets the air out of the balloon."

> **"The stakes of our universe are at once very serious and dramatic, and also very ridiculous and comedic."**
> **—Josh Heald**

Courtney Henggeler, who plays Amanda, says this is her favorite part of the role. "It's my own instinct, personally, to comment on what's happening in front of me with a bit of sarcasm, so I love that the writers give Amanda the opportunity to step into these heated, very heightened moments in the show, when fans are probably going nuts, and bring everyone down to earth a little bit." Getting to play in between Daniel and Johnny is especially exciting for Henggeler, who grew up in the '80s and witnessed the rise of *Karate Kid*-mania but was not in the original movie. "It was on constant repeat in my house growing up, and I had neighbors who took

karate because of it. *The Karate Kid* was part of our language," she says. "When I got the audition, I didn't even realize that Ralph and Billy were attached, I just thought it was another reboot. So when I got to the phase where I was reading with Ralph and Billy at my screen test, I was like 'What is this dark magic I've conjured? That's Daniel LaRusso right there, and he looks exactly the same!'"

As the seasons unfold, Amanda goes from simply being aware of her husband's karate past to getting roped into it. "I think, at first, she is above it, she knows her husband won some karate tournaments in the '80s, but she didn't understand the magnitude of it," Henggeler says. Once the LaRusso family business starts struggling because Daniel's distracted with his dojo, and then Samantha gets hurt in the high school fight because of a Cobra Kai student's dirty tactics, Amanda can no longer stand by and let boys be boys. "Her daughter is her number-one priority and the reason she gets dragged into this whole crisis. Before she could float above it—like, 'Oh we're really doing this? There's a geriatric sensei on the loose? Oh no!'—but then her daughter is physically hurt and it gets really scary for her," Henggeler says. By season three, Amanda is facing off with Kreese herself—first slapping him in the face in his dojo, and later getting served with a restraining order against him.

Though Amanda's involvement gets more serious in later seasons, Henggeler has the most fun when her character is permitted to poke fun at her husband's ridiculousness. A favorite of those moments is in season one, episode nine, when Johnny confronts Daniel at his house, and the showdown almost comes to blows. Amanda steps in right on cue: "Just a normal Saturday afternoon, a couple of grown men about to kick each other into a pool," she says. "You know, as much as I would love to watch you and your childhood karate rival duke it out, I kind of don't want to get any blood on the patio, so what do you say we try to resolve this over some breakfast instead?"

As entertaining as these moments are, the creators say they almost write themselves. "We never approach it by saying 'Let's think of the funniest scene,'" Heald says. "It's always, 'Let's write the story we're telling,' and we inevitably run into these elements that are going to be funny without even trying. The moments become the joke—they are like meta jokes in and of themselves."

Hurwitz puts it this way: "The whole concept behind the show is a comedic exercise—and yet, at the same time, we approach all the storytelling with great sincerity. It's only after the fact, when you take a step back from a scene and the entire crew is tearing up, that you're like, 'Wow, this is all rooted in a karate rivalry between characters who should have moved on by now.' Still, the original *Karate Kid* films are very meaningful to people all over the world, and very meaningful for the three of us, so we want to impact viewers' lives in the same way the movies

DANIEL'S HISTORY OF MIYAGI-DO KARATE

Welcome to Miyagi-Do Karate, home of thousands of years of history and tradition. Unlike some dojos, Miyagi-Do has deep roots. It all began with Shimpo Sensei, a fisherman who fell asleep in his boat off the coast of Okinawa and woke up off the coast of China. He returned years later with the secrets of what would become Miyagi family karate.

The Miyagi family used these techniques to fight Japanese invaders, and my own sensei, Mr. Miyagi, used them to fight for the United States in World War II. But Mr. Miyagi didn't like to fight. He always reminded me of the first rule of Miyagi-Do: Karate is for defense only. And the second rule: First learn rule number one. But anyone who mistook this for weakness was in for a big surprise. Mr. Miyagi was the strongest fighter I ever saw, and his techniques have helped me win a few fights as well.

Mr. Miyagi passed away a few years ago, but his spirit and his teachings live on at Miyagi-Do. I try every day to live up to his example and teach my students the balance, strength, and patience that will serve them both in karate and in life. It's not always easy, but I hope I'm making him proud.

impacted our lives. But at its core, it's ridiculous that we're even making the show in the first place."

The one aspect of the show that is never made light of, and always approached with genuine sincerity, is the memory of Mr. Miyagi, and his relationship with Daniel. "Daniel was a young Italian American kid from New Jersey, in a new scary environment, and had some troubles he was dealing with. He needed someone to guide him during that time in ways that perhaps his mother was unable to, so he connects with this older man from Okinawa, and they establish this surrogate father-son relationship that was really special," Hayden Schlossberg says. Mr. Miyagi was Daniel's karate sensei, sure, but the relationship went deeper than that, with Mr. Miyagi regularly sharing life lessons about balance ("Whole life have balance, everything be better"), honor ("If karate used to defend honor, defend life, karate mean something. If karate used to defend plastic metal trophy, karate no mean nothing"), fear ("It's okay to lose to opponent, it's never okay to lose to fear"), and how to live a principled life ("Never put passion in front of principle—even if you win, you'll lose"). He even took Daniel on a trip to Okinawa in *The Karate Kid II,* and the wisdom Mr. Miyagi imparted clearly shaped Daniel's transformation over the course of the movies—

THANK YOU, MR. MIYAGI

FROM RALPH MACCHIO

For me, one of the richest rewards of the *Cobra Kai* series is how it opens up the eyes of a whole new generation to the Mr. Miyagi character. Many of the younger audience members back themselves into the original *Karate Kid* film after seeing the TV series. It becomes another pathway to the origin story and broadens the legacy of Pat Morita and his brilliant portrayal of that character. I take a great deal of pride in sharing with our younger cast members a slice of Pat's wisdom and talents as we venture with each season. They become instantly engaged when I speak of the early creation of the Daniel and Miyagi dynamic and how that chemistry was born. I'll reference Pat's ability to crack a joke at any given moment (he started out as a stand-up comic) or his dedication to the authenticity of his Japanese American character. He never took the opportunity for granted, he took responsibility. He truly made it feel like he was the only person on earth to play that role. There are few characters in movies that have the impact of Mr. Miyagi. It is a joy to continue weaving

both Pat and Mr. Miyagi into the *Cobra Kai* series and story line. I believe he would be thrilled to know that he lives on in our show. His presence is felt as the legacy continues. And I channel some of it myself, being the student of yesterday stepping forward to mentor the new students of today.

A respectful handoff . . . Miyagi-Do for Life!

FROM WILLIAM ZABKA

Pat Morita and I developed a special bond during the filming of *The Karate Kid* and he was my dear friend for many years after. He was extremely kind, generous, and warm. He could put anybody at ease with his good nature and great sense of humor. We called him Uncle Pat—he called me BZ.

I had the privilege of watching him create and transform into "Mr. Miyagi" before my eyes. He liked to have fun and joke around, but when the time called, at the flip of a switch, he would become laser focused, tapped into a great well of depth and sensitivity, and "Mr. Miyagi" would come to life. He was a true artist. A total pro. A comedian with a heart of gold. A devoted father and family man. I learned so much from him.

Sadly, he left too soon, but it's comforting to know that his legacy lives on and his timeless performance as the beloved "Mr. Miyagi" is still inspiring generations of *The Karate Kid* and *Cobra Kai* fans around the world to this day.

not just in his improved karate skills, but in his maturation as a person. The incredible chemistry between Daniel and Mr. Miyagi, as well as the actors who played them, cemented the films in cinema history, even earning Pat Morita an Oscar nomination. "That connection was the lifeblood of the franchise, and I think [the fact that Pat Morita is no longer with us] was why some people were skeptical that our show could have any seriousness," Schlossberg adds. "How could we do the show without Miyagi?"

But rather than try to create *Cobra Kai* in spite of actor Pat Morita's death, the creators decided to incorporate the loss of Mr. Miyagi as a crucial story element. In season three, it's revealed that it was Mr. Miyagi who inspired Daniel to open the LaRusso Auto Group in the first place. "[When] Mr. Miyagi gave me that '47 Ford . . . that was the best day of my life," Daniel tells Amanda and his cousin Louie, who works at the dealership. "Ever since, I've been in love with cars. That's why Mr. Miyagi pushed me into sales. Wasn't my idea. I thought car salesmen were sleazy. But Mr. Miyagi told me, 'Daniel-san . . . must follow passion. Man who work for passion always richer than man who work for money.'"

"Miyagi's character plays a huge role on the show—even in his absence he's such a huge aspect of Daniel's journey," Schlossberg says. "It's that sudden

pressure to step into Miyagi's shoes and be the all-wise, all-knowing mentor to his kids, and eventually some of his kids' friends, that is weighing on Daniel and has him at this crossroads."

Macchio says his favorite episode of the entire series is in season one, when Daniel visits Mr. Miyagi's grave for the first time and opens up about his struggles—including his difficulty connecting with his kids and the anger

that has bubbled up inside him since Cobra Kai's reemergence. "I've been thinking about you a lot lately," Daniel says at the gravesite. "It's funny, when I was a kid, you seemed to always have all the answers, and I guess I thought when I got older I'd have it all figured out, too. But now I feel like I'm clueless. Makes me wonder, was it different for you or were you just better at hiding it?"

The visit reminds Daniel of Mr. Miyagi's emphasis on balance and spurs him to clear years' worth of junk out of his home training room, dust off his headband and gi, and resurrect his karate training. But the questions Daniel posed at the gravesite loom large as he takes his first unofficial karate student under his wing. Robby Keene, Johnny Lawrence's son, gets a job at LaRusso Auto Group in an effort to hurt his father, but he ends up connecting with Daniel in a powerful way. "We thought there was something very interesting about Daniel mentoring his former bully's child," Schlossberg says. "Mentorship can come from anywhere and you never know who is going to influence you in your life."

While Robby's karate studies begin unofficially—that is, not as a student of any specific dojo—his relationship with Daniel soon blossoms into a full-blown friendship, complete with all the Miyagi teachings that have gone down in pop-culture history, like "wax on, wax off," and "paint the fence," as well as a few new ones, like "jacking up the car" and "sweeping the floor." After Robby fights unaffiliated, and loses, in the season one All Valley Tournament, Daniel brings him along for the big reveal of the season one finale: Mr. Miyagi's house, where Daniel trained as a teenager, still exists, and Daniel has been holding on to it. "It's been collecting dust, as have the cars, because that space that represented something so good created a bit of a hole within Daniel when Mr. Miyagi passed," Heald says. "You get the sense that he hasn't visited it very much, because it had so much pain associated with it, and Robby was his journey back to that space."

By the start of season two, Miyagi-Do has opened its doors for business. For the indoor studio, the creators built something of a *Karate Kid* time capsule, mirroring the set of the movies. It includes a hanging scroll with the "first rule of karate" ("Karate for defense only") written in Japanese, the medal of honor Mr. Miyagi received for his service during World War II, and the original *Karate Kid*

trophy from Daniel's first All Valley victory. The biggest throwback of all? The very same 1947 Ford that Miyagi gave Daniel in the first *Karate Kid* is parked outside the dojo. The car is not a re-creation but the exact model from the movies—the *Karate Kid* producers gifted it to Macchio after filming of the first movie wrapped, and he has held on to it for three decades. When the *Cobra Kai* creators mentioned wanting to include the car on the show, Macchio offered to share the iconic ride, adding to the set's overall sentimentality.

Re-creating the outdoor Miyagi-Do space was equally important to the show's creators, but it was not an easy feat. "We had to capture the essence of the design's interior and exterior, to give the set the familiarity that the die-hard *Karate Kid* fans would expect, and still accommodate shooting for the *Cobra Kai* story," says set designer Johnny Veres. "The crew constructed the new set on our lot in Atlanta, using a somewhat landscaped area on the fringe of crew parking. Careful study of scenes from *Karate Kid I* and *II* (along with being a fan, too), helped me and my team craft a convincing Miyagi-Do, especially the exterior." In the interest of authenticity, Heald, Hurwitz, and Schlossberg wanted a real dirt driveway in the Miyagi-Do front yard, just as Mr. Miyagi had in the movies. Atlanta can be a rainy city, and it poured a lot during filming,

Set rendering depicting Samantha and Robby attempting the Miyagi-Do Wheel Technique.

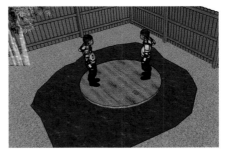

which meant shooting at Miyagi-Do turned into a muddy mess, even when it hadn't rained in three or four days. The production crew would track the dirt into the house, creating a constant cleanup problem that impacted filming. "It made you wonder why Miyagi's house wasn't more filthy," Heald jokes. There was also a patch of backyard grass that would get soaked in the rain and torn up by camera equipment. "It was a beautiful location that would look more and more horrible as the season went on," Hurwitz says.

Over time, the team worked their movie magic to give the set the same appearance without the mess. "We finally leaned into our production designer's plan to paint the driveway so it looks exactly like a dirt driveway on camera," Heald says. "Our requirement was, it has to look the same and it has to look like the movie, and it does. And now when it rains, the rain goes away and it's fine. And our greens department, which is fantastic, put down a turf that is just amazing and looks as close to real grass as you can imagine, except you're not constantly ruining it, and you're not constantly stepping in a sinkhole as you walk through that space."

At the beginning of season two, Miyagi-Do has just two students: Robby, and Samantha LaRusso, Daniel's daughter. But as the season unfolds, it grows into a full dojo—landing students like Demetri and Chris—and for much of season four it also plays host to the students of Eagle Fang, thus requiring more adaptations and improvements to the set. Because while the creators wanted the Miyagi-Do space to mirror the films, they also knew they'd have to shoot a lot of training scenes there, which meant they'd need a more elaborate set than was featured in the movies in order to move the story forward, make room for more students, and make the space feel fresh. "We had to figure out additions that we felt were organic and consistent with the Miyagi-Do we knew and loved," Hurwitz says. "Early in season two you see the balance board—the wheel where Robby and Samantha practice their floating synchronized kata—which was something we came up with in the writers' room, but also something we can believe might have been added by Mr. Miyagi in the years after the movies." To create the balance board, the production team worked with a group of engineers who had done the hydraulics on *The Fast and the Furious* franchise. The board was sturdier than it looked on-screen—so that the actors wouldn't fall into the water unless they were supposed to—and an engineer behind the scenes was tasked with manipulating the piece of wood in a way that looked like a natural reaction to the actors' moves. Another Miyagi-Do set development occurs in season four, when Hawk spearheads an undertaking to build an Okinawan sparring bridge, a symbolic gesture intended to bring the Miyagi-Do and Eagle Fang students together. "A lot of those set additions started with thinking of training or different kinds of karate lessons," Hurwitz says. "We are trying to solve problems, but the solutions always come from looking for something that feels true to Mr. Miyagi's spirit."

Macchio says stepping into that yard for the first time was surprisingly emotional. "When I first walked into the Miyagi-Do backyard, I just stood there for a nanosecond and it hit me that this space, for me, is where the magic would happen. It was nostalgic, on a personal level, because I felt the presence of John Avildsen [*The Karate Kid* director], and Robert Kamen, the writer of the original film, and certainly Pat Morita and his iconic performance as Mr. Miyagi. I just had that rush of emotion and I got a little welled up in my eyes, thinking about how a lot of those people aren't here anymore. But also, on the flip side, how they are shining down on this whole universe in the fact that this saga continues, and we continue to tell these stories. Without them, we're not here."

Macchio says it's exciting to pass the Miyagi-Do torch to the next generation. "My favorite thing to do in this show is work with our young cast," he notes. And the feeling is mutual—the young actors all say they are thrilled to be performing alongside the original Karate Kid. "I remember getting a call from the Karate Kid himself, Ralph Macchio, congratulating me and welcoming me to the universe," Tanner Buchanan, who plays Robby, says of joining the cast. "I didn't know what to expect, but it has been amazing." In fact, the first two Miyagi-Do students had an instant connection with their TV sensei. "We saw immediately that there was this bond happening between Ralph and Mary Mouser, who plays Samantha. And then quickly thereafter, as soon as Tanner Buchanan's character, Robby Keene, came into the Miyagi-Do folds, there was almost this Miyagi-Daniel thing happening, where there was this bond and all three of them were of the same mindset," says Heald. "It almost felt like they

LOVE LETTERS FROM THE PAST

Dated 5/15/94

Yukie,

Hello from Boston! I did not expect to be here for long, but there is someone I have been helping. Her name is Julie Pierce. She is the granddaughter of a man I served with during the war.

Julie-san says I don't understand girls. I fear she is right. Do you have any advice for me?

Love,
Nariyoshi Miyagi

———————

Dated 9/23/06

Yukie,

Although we have been away from each other for far too long, I can still picture you clearly every day. Each time I read your letters, I hear your voice. Some days, I think I am the luckiest man in all the world. How else could I explain my many blessings? I have friends, family, and best of all, I have love.

Ever since we were little, when you smiled at me, so shy, I have loved you. One good thing came out of our time apart—I got to fall in love with you twice in one lifetime.

I would like to write more, but it will have to wait. I hear Samantha-san calling for me. She has already been asking me if I will help her make a Halloween costume. It is over a month away!

Love,
Nariyoshi Miyagi

————————————

Dated 11/8/11

My Sweetheart Yukie,

I am sorry it has been a long time since my last letter. I am so happy to hear Kanhizakura is in good health. I am sorry to tell you that I am back in the hospital. Please, do not worry. There is nothing to do, except watch TV and think. Think about family. Think about us. Think about where I have been. Think about where I am going.

In life, I have always looked for signs to show me the right way. But I got lost. Until I met Daniel-san. His strong heart, strong chi, and loyalty and love for those around him is a guiding light to me. I am very proud for the man he has become, even though he still has a hard head.

I never thought I would have a family again. Daniel-san has welcomed me into his family and he has passed on what I teach him in Miyagi-Do to his daughter. Samantha makes me feel like I am her tanmee.

In life we always lose our way . . . but it is people, not the signs, that guide us back to the right path. Do you like that, Yukie? I heard that in a car commercial.

Love,
Nariyoshi Miyagi

were a unique little family unto themselves on set, in terms of the way they approached their work and asked questions and prepared. It was interesting to see some mini-Ralphs sprout up around us."

Of course, Daniel's attempts to establish himself as a sensei don't always go smoothly. He reiterates the Miyagi-Do philosophies—primarily the idea that karate is "for defense only"—but he realizes early on that even though he learned from Mr. Miyagi, it doesn't mean he can replace him. "I enjoy seeing Daniel struggle with that, when he has to figure out his own Miyagi-isms and pinpoint how to pass on a lesson or a piece of wisdom," Macchio says. "It's not as easy as it looks, and he has his own LaRusso version of what he gained from Mr. Miyagi, but it doesn't always work so well." When a fight in the school between the Miyagi-Do and Cobra Kai students leaves Samantha scarred and traumatized, and sends Robby on the run after pushing Miguel over a stairwell railing, Daniel is sure he's in over his head. It's not until he takes a trip to Okinawa in season three that he gets a sense of his full inheritance, and realizes that even Mr. Miyagi didn't have it all figured out. He reconnects with Kumiko, his love interest from *The Karate Kid II*, who shares with him a letter Mr. Miyagi wrote to her aunt a week before he died. "In life I have always looked for signs to show me the right way when I got lost . . . until I met Daniel-san," his letter states. "His strong heart, strong chi, and loyalty and love for those around

him is a guiding light to me. I am very proud for the man he has become, even though he still has a hard head. I never thought I would have a family again. Daniel-san has welcomed me into his family and he has passed on what I teach him in Miyagi-Do to his daughter. Samantha makes me feel like I am her [grandfather]. . . . In life we always lose our way, but it is people, not the signs, that guide us back to the right path."

Bringing the series back to Okinawa, and even filming some of those scenes in Japan, was on the creators' radars since they conceived of the series. "We didn't want to throw everything into season one, but we started thinking early on about where the series could go in the future," Schlossberg says. "Going into season three, we knew we wanted to have some of the story take place in Okinawa, but the challenge of our show is always the budget. The *Karate Kid* movies were bigger budget, plus we have multiple episodes that our budget needs to cover. So we realized pretty quickly that the only way we could top the movie was to be more authentic and actually go to Okinawa. The original movie built an enormous set in Hawaii and it looked cool, but we could add some coolness of our own by going to the location."

Like Miyagi before him, Daniel is ultimately motivated by the urge to connect with the people he loves. Supporting and protecting his family is his guiding light, and, after finding newfound clarity during his visit to Okinawa, Daniel realizes Miyagi-Do must evolve accordingly. Even if that eventually means partnering with his one-time enemy, Johnny, in order to defeat the ultra-nemesis, John Kreese, and take down Cobra Kai once and for all. "I'm absolutely thrilled with the chemistry that Billy and I have. Those scenes are such highlights for me each season, when we're together," Macchio says. "There's such a rich history we each bring, having both been connected to the movie, so it's super emotional and nostalgic, and at the same time, it's still a karate soap opera about two guys fighting as if there's a religious war in the San Fernando Valley. It's gloriously ridiculous."

03
THE APARTMENT COMPLEX

"YOU CAN'T LET THE MISTAKES OF THE PAST DETERMINE YOUR FUTURE"

Welcome to the Reseda Apartment Complex. The individual units may not have much to offer—two or three small bedrooms, a tiny kitchen off the living area, outdated finishes—but home is what you make it, right? In Unit 2, Johnny Lawrence, a resident for over ten years, has what you'd describe (generously, perhaps) as a bachelor pad. Limited furniture, paper plates, bare walls—except for a picture of three chicks at a pool—and a mostly empty fridge. But a few doors down, you'll find the Diaz family— hard-working mother, doting but quick-witted grandmother, and eager teenage son Miguel—who've created a colorful and homey space where

any family can build a future. The close living quarters means you'll never know who you'll meet or who's just around the corner.

One such relationship is the backbone of the entire series. When Miguel and Johnny first meet, Miguel just wants to ask a question about the water pressure. He's new in town, having just moved from Riverside, and his family is excited about their new home. "Listen, Menudo," Johnny says in response. "I've lived in this shithole for over ten years. The pipes don't work, the fountain's full of piss, and the only good thing about living here is that I don't have to talk to anybody. So nice knowing you." It's a rocky start, but a familiar one for *Karate Kid* fans. After all, run-down apartment complexes have a history of launching intergenerational friendships in the Miyagi-verse. The South Seas complex, also in Reseda, where Daniel LaRusso lived in high school and Mr. Miyagi worked as the maintenance man, is where the two first connected. Mirroring that setup in *Cobra Kai* was an easy choice for the series' creators. "It was really about putting present-day Johnny in 1984 Daniel's situation. We gave Johnny the downstairs apartment rather than upstairs, but other than that it is a similarly designed building," Josh Heald says. "Though this time there's no maintenance man on site who's keeping it up, at least not that we've met."

Though the apartment complex serves as a throwback to the original films, it also brings the series into the modern day, introducing a more accurate and inclusive representation of the kinds of people who might actually reside there. "The San Fernando Valley has a huge Hispanic population," Hayden Schlossberg says. (As of the 2019 US census, the Valley was 42 percent Hispanic.) "So we were happy to show that. And we thought it would be so cool

"I've lived in this shithole for over ten years. The pipes don't work, the fountain's full of piss, and the only good thing about living here is that I don't have to talk to anybody. So nice knowing you."
—Johnny Lawrence

for the Latin audience to finally have their own Karate Kid hero." Because while much of *Cobra Kai* is about nostalgia and wink-wink '80s references, it ultimately wants to reflect the universe its characters (and viewers) live in.

Other than Pat Morita's character, *The Karate Kid* was noticeably lacking when it came to diversity in its cast—a flaw *Cobra Kai* works hard to improve upon.

But despite *The Karate Kid's* shortcomings in the representation department, the connection between Daniel and Mr. Miyagi relies on the fact that they share and educate each other about their distinct cultures. Vanessa Rubio, the actress who plays Miguel's mother (and Johnny's eventual girlfriend), Carmen, says the inclusion of the Diaz family furthers that tradition. "One of the reasons why *The Karate Kid* has such an enduring legacy is the bridging of virtues that are embodied in different cultures—how one character teaches the other and how each is strengthened by this ability to learn from one another," she says.

MIGUEL DIAZ

DOJO: Eagle Fang, Cobra Kai (former)

ALLIES: Demetri Alexopoulos, Hawk, Samantha LaRusso

NEMESES: Robby Keene, Kyler Park

CHARACTER PHILOSOPHY:

"There's no honor in being merciless."

LOVE INTERESTS: Samantha LaRusso, Tory Nichols (former)

FAMILY: Carmen Diaz (mother), Rosa Diaz (grandmother)

"It's an honor to play Carmen, and for her and her family to represent Latinos, because they come with their own set of virtues and strengths, which are exemplified in their family unit. Their way of working in the world is unique to them, and it is something that they bring from Ecuador. It involves a strong sense of family, community, and spirituality, not to mention a good sense of humor."

For Carmen and her family, much like Lucille and Daniel before them, the apartment complex represents the chance at a better life. As Carmen reveals to Johnny in season one, she left Ecuador when she was pregnant because "I learned the truth about my husband's job. Let's just say he was a very bad man. I had to get far away from him." The Diaz family has been moving around ever since. When Johnny says he's sorry to hear it, Carmen clarifies. "Don't be sorry," she says. "I moved on long ago. You can't let the mistakes of the past determine your future." For the Diaz family, the Reseda apartment complex is a step on their continued journey to that brighter future. "This new home provides a sense of safety and stability for Carmen and her family that she was seeking for a good while," Rubio says. "It's an opportunity to live a life that has more stable ground—and an opportunity to stop running. It's also proof that the small day-to-day things Carmen has always done—working, studying, saving up—have paid off. She's finally able to have a stable home with her family, and with that comes the ability to build relationships in the complex. The Diaz family likes a sense of community. They are the type to know their neighbors and try to support them, they've just been waiting for the stable ground to do so."

But just as the apartment complex is a sign of transience and upward mobility for Carmen and her family, for Johnny, it signifies a downward spiral. "It's just four walls and a roof," says Heald. "He's a man without a positive influence in his life, living on limited means and just getting through the day, eating his bologna and watching whatever's on basic broadcast television. Then here comes Miguel and his family, and it's a better place than where they lived in Riverside, and this could be the first step on the ladder of an aspirational climb for this kid."

The design of the apartment complex set, and the individual apartments within it, took this symbolism into account. "We put Johnny in a very simple

apartment that you might see in Reseda today. It's a little bit run-down, it was probably built in the 1960s or '70s, and it's unimpressive to look at, even on camera," Heald says. "Whenever we're filming there, our production designer is wringing his hands a little bit because he wants to make something beautiful. But it *is* beautiful for what it is—Johnny's not going to have great art on the walls. He's going to put up a framed poster that he may have won at the carnival twenty-five years ago." The Diazes' apartment, on the other hand, has more warmth, and depicts a home that has been built with loving attention. "We took some liberty and made that space slightly bigger to accentuate it on camera, but really we just filled it with a little more life," Heald says. "There are some plants, and some real intention regarding what goes on the walls and how things are organized. Johnny's apartment, at least at the start, takes on the conditions of the life he has created for himself, whereas Miguel and Rosa and Carmen are not looking at this complex as some crummy place where you just get through the day. It's a home, and it feels like a family lives there."

The *Cobra Kai* production crew built two different sets to portray the apartment complex—an outside set, which gives the ability for cars to pull up, and also has the area with the trash cans where Miguel and Johnny first interact, and an indoor one that connects to the apartments themselves and lets the characters walk back and forth between them. The exterior shots, that show the outside of the building, are of a real apartment building in the Valley (at 18555 Burbank Boulevard in Tarzana, to be exact).

While the Reseda complex gets the most airtime, it's not the only apartment in the series that tells a larger story and helps viewers understand the characters who live there. Robby Keene and Tory Nichols are both introduced as teenagers with tough exteriors, but their home situations are proof of a deeper and more complex tale. Robby lives in an apartment with his mother, Shannon (played by Diora Baird), an alcoholic who mostly leaves Robby to fend for himself so she can go to happy hours and pick up men. The first time that viewers see Robby in his apartment, in episode four of the first season, he's cutting school and smoking weed in his living room with two friends. In episode five, when he tries to schedule one-on-one time at the apartment with his mom, she rejects the offer in favor of a night on the town. It's clear Robby is longing for a positive adult influence in his life, but his mother seems unlikely to step up to the plate. His father, Johnny, *does* want to, but, as Robby reminds him, he's sixteen years too late. Early in season two, Robby's home troubles

PRODUCTION DESIGNER RYAN BERG

S ince season one, Ryan Berg has been creating the spaces that set the tone for the *Cobra Kai* universe. From the dojos to the high school to Johnny's and Daniel's homes, Berg—whose production designer credits include the FX comedy *Better Things* and the TV series of *Wet Hot American Summer*—leads the stellar team that designs and builds the signature sets. Here he opens up about how he conceived some of the show's most notable backdrops.

The Cobra Kai dojo space goes under a number of transformations during the series, first under Johnny, then under Kreese, then Terry Silver and Kreese. How did you change the space and the set design to reflect those transformations?
For the first season, I designed Johnny's Cobra Kai with a really basic and cheap mini-mall style. It was what Johnny could afford. When Kreese entered the picture, the space became a mutation of Johnny's original dojo—Johnny's dojo but harder and grungier. The raw space that we added showed that tougher edge that Kreese brought, and made the space even meaner. In the fourth season with Terry Silver's dojo there is a major transformation of what we have known as a dojo.

What went into designing the apartment complex, specifically the interiors of Johnny's apartment and the Diaz apartment? What were the differences in how you approached each space?
I love sets like the Reseda Heights apartments. I really like the challenge of making something look run-down and believable, but also good-looking on camera. Johnny was a bare-bones, down-on-his-luck guy and required little, if any, decor in his world.

With the exception of the posters on his wall—which he sees as cool—the rest of the place is utility living only. The colors were the bland neutral that are typical of lower-rent apartments.

For Carmen's apartment, I wanted the same layout but to dress it more like a home. I placed nice but modest items around to create the vibe of a good home life for Miguel.

Some spaces in the Miyagi-verse, like Miyagi-Do, are "sacred ground." How did you use the original films as inspiration, and how did you adapt the spaces to work for the new show?

Miyagi's house is the most sacred space in the *Karate Kid* universe and I had to dig deep into the movies to piece it all together. I learned that from the first *Karate Kid* film to the second, they took some artistic liberties which, of course, allowed me to do the same. My main goal was to make the front and back of the house match up as best I could, and then worry separately about the interior sets, since individual spaces didn't necessarily need to add up. I took elements from the interiors shown in the movies and added those into rooms we needed for the series.

worsen when his mom heads to Mexico with a new boyfriend, leaving Robby with no food, unpaid bills, and no electricity. It's a life that informs so many of Robby's decisions throughout the series—from his interest in LaRusso Auto Group to his eventual dedication to Kreese and Cobra Kai. "Robby has had to take care of himself basically since he was born," Buchanan says. "His dad was never there for him and neither was his mom, even if she was there physically. He always did what he needed to do to survive, but it isn't the way he wants to live. Robby has always wanted to be a good person and be successful, and he doesn't mind working hard, he just never had the right guidance." As Robby gets older and is let down by more people, he starts to believe the only person he can trust is himself. "By the beginning of season four, I think Robby's motivations are to prove everyone wrong," Buchanan says. "Robby wants to show that he can be successful and on top of the world all by himself." Being constantly left behind by the people he needs most takes its toll on Robby, and in the end of season four viewers get to see just how worn down he really is. In the season finale, he finds Johnny in the Cobra Kai dojo and reveals that all he wanted as a kid was a mentor, and that his father's constant screwups produced a teenager full of anger. It's a vulnerable moment for Robby, who is yearning for nothing more than a father figure and a secure home environment. When Johnny tries to accept the blame for his mistakes as a father, Robby indicates he may be ready to put all his rage behind him. "I'm sick of blaming you, Dad," he says through tears. Still, for most of the series, Robby's home life is neither safe nor comfortable, so he goes out of his way to prove he doesn't need those things anyway.

Possessing a similar outlook is Tory Nichols, a Cobra Kai student and Kreese devotee who joins the series in season two. When she's first introduced, viewers meet a tough fighter who has no problems stealing a bottle of vodka from a country club or shoving Samantha LaRusso into a buffet table. Over time, however, it's revealed that much of her worldview is shaped by her family's experiences struggling to make ends meet—her mother was fired for stealing after taking home leftovers from the restaurant where she works, even though they would have been thrown out at the end of the day. For Tory, this single instance represents the harsh realities of life for those who aren't rich and

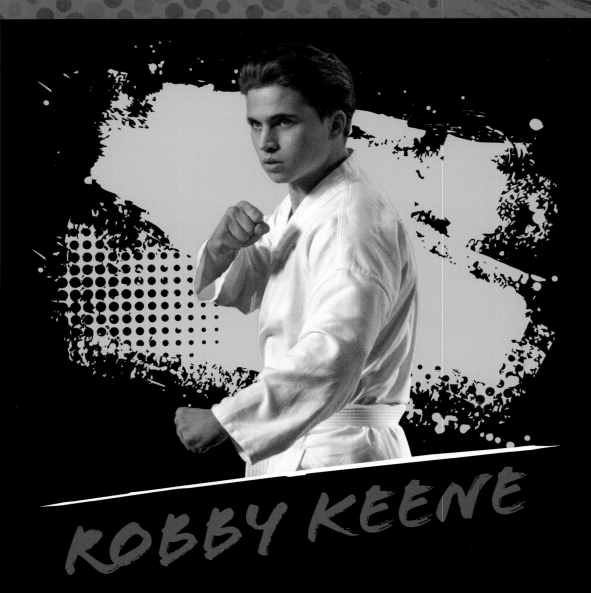

ROBBY KEENE

DOJO: Cobra Kai, Miyagi-Do (former)

ALLIES: Kenny Payne, Tory Nichols, Samantha LaRusso (former)

NEMESIS: Miguel Diaz

CHARACTER PHILOSOPHY: "It doesn't matter which way you fight, as long as it works."

LOVE INTERESTS: Tory Nichols, Samantha LaRusso (former)

FAMILY: Johnny Lawrence (father), Shannon Keene (mother)

privileged. "The world shows no mercy," she tells Miguel in season two. "Some people have it good, but the rest of us, we have to fight for every inch of what's ours. Not just to score a point . . . for everything." This attitude is what spurs Tory to start the epic brawl at the high school that closes season two. After she sees Samantha LaRusso and Miguel, who by that point is Tory's boyfriend, kiss at a party, she decides to fight for what's hers.

> **"The world shows no mercy. Some people have it good, but the rest of us, we have to fight for every inch of what's ours. Not just to score a point . . . for everything."**
> **—Tory Nichols**

In season three, even more of Tory's home life is revealed—she is caring for her mother, who is on dialysis, and her little brother at the run-down apartment complex where they live. She's working two jobs in an (unsuccessful) effort to make rent. In the season's second episode, her landlord comes after her for a late payment, not-so-subtly propositioning her and offering to forgive the overdue rent in exchange for a late-night rendezvous. It's not until Kreese finds out about Tory's home life, and takes care of her rent predicament by nearly cutting off the landlord's finger, that Tory finally finds someone who will look out for her. His methods may be a bit twisted, but that doesn't stop Tory from feeling a connection to him. "Kreese sees Tory as a great fighter, and he's protected her from her creepy landlord who tried to take advantage of her. Maybe he sees a part of himself in her, I don't know, but he's taken her in and she's never had that before," says Peyton List, who plays Tory. "He has become her mentor—the biggest parental figure in her life and her biggest role model. He actually sees something good in her." List says she can't help but hold a special place in her heart for the villainous Kreese. "Oddly enough, I've gotten so involved in justifying everything Tory does that when I think about Kreese, and his backstory, I'm just like, 'I love him so much.'"

In playing Tory and trying to communicate her motivations—specifically the desire to have an adult see the good in her—List says she often draws on what she's witnessed firsthand. "Kids really just want someone to see something in them, especially when they're hurting because of things at home. I've seen a lot

of Torys at public schools growing up in New York. You see people coming from broken homes and it's not the kids that are the problem, it's the environment." In Tory's case, she's equally motivated to show *herself* that she's good enough, and that has to be done on the karate mat, because no matter how hard she tries, she doesn't get it at home. List explains it this way: "Tory wants to prove to herself that she can keep up with all these other kids who had everything given to them. She's not a bad person, she has good in her, she's just been beaten down so much that she makes bad decisions."

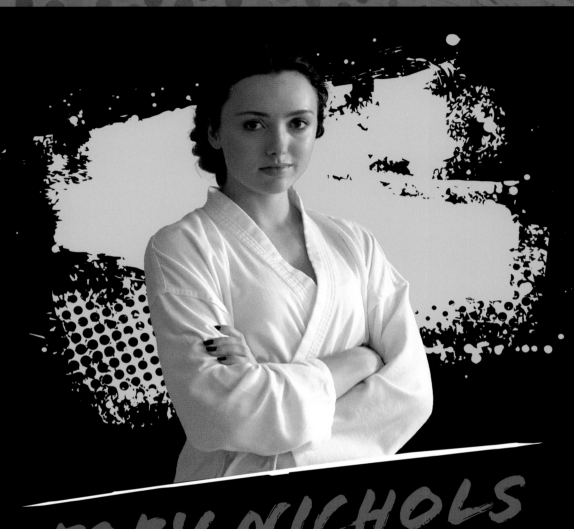

TORY NICHOLS

DOJO: Cobra Kai

ALLIES: Robby Keene, John Kreese

NEMESIS: Samantha LaRusso

CHARACTER PHILOSOPHY:

"The world shows no mercy. So why should we?"

LOVE INTERESTS: Robby Keene, Miguel Diaz (former)

FAMILY: Mother, Brandon (brother), Aunt Kandace

Tory's Rules for Battle

1. Don't wait for your enemy to attack. If you let someone have the upper hand, you've already lost. Act, don't react.

2. Know who your friends are. A lot of people will just stab you in the back. Most of the time, you can't trust anyone but yourself. But when someone does right by you, appreciate it—it won't happen often.

3. Don't always fight fair. Yeah, maybe in a tournament you have a referee to protect you, but guess what? Off the mat, life isn't fair. If you always play by the rules, you get screwed.

4. Be ready to earn what's yours. Sure, some people get everything handed to them. Not all of us are that lucky. If you're not ready to beat everyone and everything in your way, you'll never be a winner.

5. Never back down. Lose a fight? That's just motivation to win the next one. Nobody can make you a loser unless you let them. Keep fighting till the end.

04

THE HIGH SCHOOL

"BACK IN MY DAY, IF WE WANTED TO TEASE SOMEONE, WE DID IT TO THEIR FACE"

I f the West Valley High of 1984 and 2018 have anything in common, it's the fact that bullies still run the hallways, the Halloween dance is still tradition, and where you sit in the lunchroom is forever a tell-tale sign of your social standing. The differences, however, are vast. Rather than the sexy nurse costumes of years past, the school counselor recommends wearing a "gender-neutral hospital worker" costume to the dance. Karate remains the fighting method of choice, but now the girls are in on the action. And though the students from the different dojos generally stick together, West Valley is the one place where these kids have no choice but to

DENIZENS OF THE DOJOS

It wouldn't be a karate war without soldiers on both sides. Meet the karate kids (and one somewhat misguided adult) who fill out the ranks of Cobra Kai, Miyagi-Do, and Eagle Fang.

AISHA was Johnny's second student—and the one who convinced him that girls can fight, despite their "brittle bird bones." Johnny taught Aisha how to fight back against her bullies and take charge of her life.

BERT joined Johnny's Cobra Kai and later followed him to Eagle Fang. Bert might look small, but he packs a punch and even managed to land a point on a fighter three times his size at the All Valley.

NATE, Bert's on-and-off rival, defected from Cobra Kai to Miyagi-Do in season two. Don't underestimate him—he absolutely owned the kata section at the All Valley.

CHRIS and **MITCH** are wrestling fans who join Johnny's Cobra Kai in season two. Their bond is broken when Chris defects to Miyagi-Do and they end up on opposite sides of the school fight. But they reunite at the end of season three and fight together against Kreese's Cobras. Mitch is sometimes known as Penis Breath—but only his fellow Eagle Fangs can call him that.

DEVON is the most badass girl Johnny has ever met and becomes Eagle Fang's star female fighter. Devon's new to karate (Johnny first spots her when she goes off on an opponent at a debate meet) but she learns quickly and isn't afraid to call Johnny out.

KENNY is the new kid in the Valley in season four who finds himself the target of bullying by none other than Anthony LaRusso. Kenny's desperate to fight back and ends up as Robby's mentee in Cobra Kai. Robby just wants to help the kid, but, when Kenny embraces Cobra Kai's aggression and violence, Robby finds that being a role model is harder than he thought.

STINGRAY—the man, the myth, the legend—is Cobra Kai's oldest student. He might not have friends his own age, but that just gives him more time to dedicate to his dojo. His eagerness to prove himself as a Cobra Kai constantly lands him in some legal hot water, from his participation in the huge school fight to his false testimony against Kreese.

coexist. "We knew viewers needed to see the haves mingle with the have-nots and see the discrimination that takes place between the two, as in instances like the Halloween fight," Josh Heald says. "That's what we were marching toward in season one at the halfway point, with Miguel and Kyler switching their power dynamic after the fight in the lunchroom." In fact, a handful of the series' most memorable showdowns have taken place at West Valley—most notably the aforementioned lunchroom fight where Miguel faced off with Kyler and his gang of bullies, and the epic 10-minute season two finale fight, whose consequences reverberate all the way through season four.

The actors who play the high school students—most of whom are now in their early twenties—were born decades after the *Karate Kid* films came out; a number of them admit they didn't grasp how beloved the Miyagi-verse really was when they signed on for *Cobra Kai*. "My dad showed me the movies when I was eight," Jacob Bertrand, who plays Hawk, says. "There were a slew of movies he wanted to show me before I was thirteen—you know, 'Before you become a man, these are the movies you need to see.' *The Karate Kid* films were a part of that list, so when I was auditioning for the role I knew it was really cool, but I didn't realize how big it would be." Gianni DeCenzo, who plays ultra-witty fan-favorite Demetri, had also seen the movies, but, like Bertrand, he says he didn't anticipate how rabid the *Cobra Kai* fan base would be. "In hindsight, it's a follow-up to *Karate Kid* so I probably should have realized it would be a big deal, but I was sixteen at the time. I was like 'Oh, I'm going to play a nerd? Cool, I can do that. I'm a geek at heart.'"

Not knowing the extent of the trilogy's impact was ultimately helpful for a number of the young actors. "My mom always talked about *The Karate Kid* when I was growing up, so I was familiar with it, but I didn't really appreciate or realize just how big it was, which I guess is a good way to get into it—not really knowing much, so not being too nervous," Peyton List says. DeCenzo echoes this: "If I had known how much scrutiny season one would be under—because with any reboot people always expect the worst—I probably would have been more tense on day one of filming." He was tense enough as is. The first time DeCenzo met William Zabka was the day they filmed one of their most memorable scenes. "The very first time I met him, I called his character a Nazi and then he flipped me," DeCenzo says. "So that was interesting."

The cast members largely credit William Zabka and Ralph Macchio for allowing each young actor to find their place in the new series, rather than priming them for the cult fan base they'd ultimately encounter. "They really didn't talk to us about how big the movies used to be or what to expect," List says. "They come in every day and they're very professional—they're really good role models for me. Just watching them work, I learn so much. Ralph, most of the time, he tries to be like 'Oh, I'm just an old guy, I had my day. I'm done.' And I'm like, 'Uh, Ralph, you're in great shape. I see you in training, stop being modest.'"

Zabka admits he's been tempted to dispense advice to his younger counterparts, but has refrained from doing so out of respect to them. "I didn't want to overwhelm them and say 'Hey, look what you're a part of,' and have that be in their heads," he says. "Their job as actors is to do their homework and connect with the roles, so I was more interested in creating an environment of, 'This is a new show, these are new characters, we're all starting with this together.' It's a team thing. I don't go giving out advice unless it's asked for personally, because everyone has their own process."

Still, Zabka says it was fun to watch the actors discover the Miyagi-verse in

SAMANTHA LARUSSO

DOJO: Miyagi-Do

ALLIES: Aisha Robinson, Demetri Alexopoulos, Miguel Diaz,
Robby Keene (former), Moon

NEMESIS: Tory Nichols

CHARACTER PHILOSOPHY: "Everyone has a sob story.
That doesn't give you the right to be a bully."

LOVE INTERESTS: Miguel Diaz, Robby Keene (former), Kyler Park (former)

FAMILY: Daniel LaRusso (father), Amanda LaRusso (mother), Anthony LaRusso
(brother), Louie LaRusso (cousin), Lucille LaRusso (grandmother)

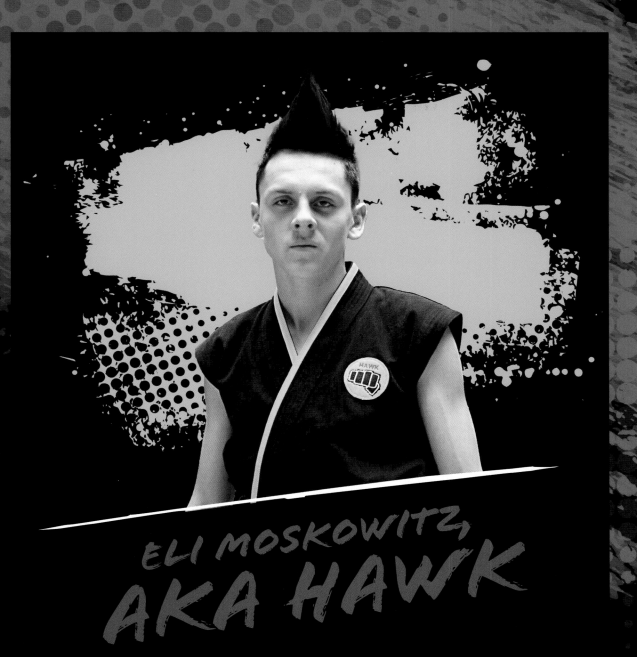

ELI MOSKOWITZ, AKA HAWK

DOJO: Miyagi-Do, Eagle Fang (former), Cobra Kai (former)

ALLIES: Demetri Alexopoulos, Miguel Diaz

NEMESES: Kyler Park, Demetri (former), Robby Keene (former)

CHARACTER PHILOSOPHY: "Fear does not exist."

LOVE INTEREST: Moon

the early days of filming season one. "A lot of the cast—Xolo Maridueña [who plays Miguel], Mary Mouser [Samantha], Tanner Buchanan [Robby], and Nichole Brown, who plays Aisha—they would have movie nights and brush up on their *Karate Kid* trivia and I would get text messages saying things like 'I'm totally team Johnny! I'm totally Cobra Kai!' so it happened organically. And it was really fun to watch them discover this world, because it wasn't a film for their generation. They had their own movies. So for them to go back and discover this and *see* what they were becoming a part of, on their own, it was pretty great." Of course, for the young cast, becoming a part of the Miyagi-verse would mean becoming fighters themselves. Though some of them had taken martial arts classes as kids, the young actors were largely inexperienced in that regard. But that would change as they started working with their stunt doubles and training for fight scenes—a necessary, if not entirely expected, part of the gig.

Bringing West Valley High into the twenty-first century—"Gender-neutral hospital workers" and all—meant writing dialogue and creating story lines that are true to teen life today, a feat that could have proved challenging for Josh Heald, Jon Hurwitz, and Hayden Schlossberg, all of whom are in their forties. But the guys credit their long-standing friendship, which started in their own teenage years, with helping them get into the high school mentality. "Because we have some shared experiences from our youth, we were able to tap into those memories and those dynamics," Hurwitz says. "In many ways, our relationship is still the same as it was when we were teens, so that mindset is more on the forefront for us than it would be otherwise." Hurwitz and Schlossberg went to high school together, and even back then they paid close attention to the different personality types they encountered, creating story lines about other kids. "We were friends on the debate team, and we gave every person from other schools—students *and* coaches—nicknames at debate meets," Hurwitz says. "They all had imagined backstories, or we got to know them and their real backstories, but they were characters in our own universe, and they were our own villains, because we were competing against them. We'd have these rivals, these battles, and the kids from other schools would walk in and they were little badasses in their own way—we were all a bunch of nerds in suits—but we'd come up with these in-depth ideas as to what was going on in their lives."

And the show's creators aren't the only ones who pen the episodes and come up with story lines. "There's a room full of writers of all ages with different experiences of their own," Hurwitz says. "It's a great collaboration where people are throwing out all sorts of ideas. What's great about a writers' room is that everyone is telling stories from their youth. And some of that stuff works its way into the show."

But not all story lines are cut out of high school yearbooks. Inspiration can come from any number of unexpected places, and the creators say they're often surprised at what can spark an idea. They point to the HBO show *Oz,* about the inner workings of a prison, as one such example. As longtime fans of the show, they loved the idea of creating similar dynamics in a high school environment. They imagined how West Valley, with its rivalries and hierarchies and love triangles, could feel like life or death for its students, even if most of their problems can be characterized as run-of-the-mill high school drama.

Some of the *Cobra Kai* teen rivalries really do rise to the level of life and death—just look at Miguel and Robby, whose feud for much of season two leads to a fight that ends with Miguel temporarily paralyzed and Robby in juvie—but plenty of the bullying comes in less physically violent, if equally detrimental, forms. Kyler mocks Eli for his cleft lip; Yasmine calls Aisha a pig on social media; Eli, in season two, by now fully transformed into Hawk, belittles Demetri for being weak; Tory provokes Sam by calling her a bitch over the school loudspeaker. In *Cobra Kai,* bullying is shown from every angle—what it's like to be bullied, but also what it's like to be the bully, and why or how someone might transition from a victim into the aggressor. These different perspectives are depicted most clearly in Miguel, Demetri, and Eli, who, when the series begins, are all sitting at the "nerd" table in the cafeteria. That changes when Miguel starts learning karate, and over the course of the first two seasons, the three friends follow very different paths. As a result of his lessons with Johnny, Miguel gains enough confidence to stand up to Kyler when he harasses Samantha in front of their classmates. "When he sees Sam getting bullied in the cafeteria, Miguel finally feels able to say something about it," Maridueña says. "He didn't actually think he could take down all those guys, but he had just enough confidence to be able to say something in Sam's defense, and then it was like his fight-or-flight instincts took over." From that point on, Miguel becomes more self-assured, though he still generally chooses integrity and humanity over violence.

Eli, on the other hand, plunges deep into the dark side when he becomes Hawk, changing from a meek, quiet kid to a straight-up bully who takes his newfound persona too far. "Mentally, Eli is not the strongest. He was bullied his whole life, and he never learned how to stick up for himself. He didn't know how to set moral boundaries or stand his ground," Bertrand says. The actor notes that he, too, was bullied a lot while growing up, and uses those experiences when inhabiting his character. "I try to bring back all those thoughts and emotions from when I was a kid," he says. "You feel so small, and nothing feels like it's in your control. I didn't have the crazy mohawk, or the flipping the script moment, but I gained confidence and built my self-esteem as I grew up, so I just multiply that by twelve when I have a mohawk in the show."

When Eli becomes Hawk, "he has everything he ever wanted," Bertrand points out—strength, power, attention—and he lets that all go to his head (pun intended!). During seasons one and two, the once-tortured kid becomes the torturer. It's a close-up look at one of the overarching questions of the show—*What makes a bully?*—and Bertrand says his favorite moments are

Hawk's Most Badass Moves

- Flip the script—You're only a loser if you let yourself be a loser. Sick of being bullied and laughed at? Make a change. Prove that you're a badass and make sure everyone knows it.

- Know who you are—People will give you all kinds of labels: bully, nerd, the kid with the lip. All that shit is just noise. You decide who you are.

- Don't be a dick—Yeah, it's easy to get carried away and take things too far. But being a badass doesn't mean being a bully. Believe me, I learned this the hard way—don't let your toughness and kickass moves go to your head.

- Tornado Axe Kick—It's not all about confidence and life lessons. To be a badass, you need some seriously hardcore moves, and this one is SICK. I'm still working on it, but when I master it, the Valley better watch out!

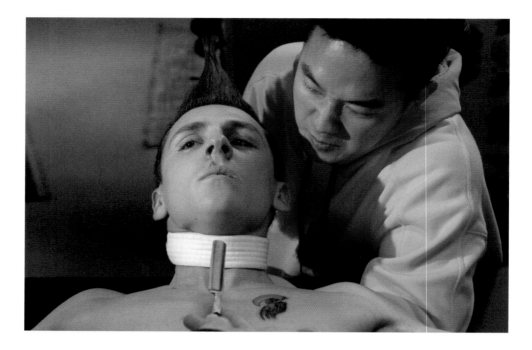

when he's tasked with reminding viewers that Hawk is still Eli deep down; you just have to comb through the hairdo a bit. "I love getting to show the tics and insecurities of Eli while I'm still being Hawk," he says. "Like during the party scene in season two, when Moon starts kissing that other girl while he's talking to Demetri. He's so uncomfortable and insecure, and I love how the writers are always bringing up that snapshot of Eli in Hawk's body." The task of uniting Hawk and Eli becomes even more important in season four, when the Cobra Kais shave Hawk's head as part of an ongoing pretournament prank war. Now the character resembles the Eli viewers once knew, but with a tougher interior. "It was fun getting to explore the question of 'who is Hawk without the 'hawk?'" Bertrand says.

One thing Hawk had long before the haircut? A best friend in Demetri, who, for as long as he can, just tries to stay far away from any fighting. He doesn't want to kick ass, he doesn't want to pick on other people, he just wants to lay low, get good grades, and go unnoticed so he can escape high school unscathed. As he explains to Miguel before an SAT practice test: "I've got to do well on these so I do well on the actual test, so I get into a good college, which will lead to a good internship, then a high-paying job, and then, after a couple

DEMETRI ALEXOPOULOS

DOJO: Miyagi-Do

ALLIES: Hawk, Miguel Diaz, Samantha LaRusso

NEMESIS: Hawk (former)

CHARACTER PHILOSOPHY:

"I just want to show I can fight back."

LOVE INTEREST: Yasmine

promotions, I should have enough confidence to get a super-hot girl. You've got the karate thing. I've gotta play the long game." It's one of many lines that establish Demetri as the wise outside observer to the inner world of karate chaos in the early days. And just as Amanda LaRusso so often speaks aloud what the audience is thinking, so too does Demetri, calling out the absurdities of a world where karate violence runs rampant. "You know when you're watching a show and you scream at the TV, like, 'Don't go through the door!' And you're so frustrated because they can't hear you? Demetri is that character who says, 'Hey, maybe we shouldn't go through that door,'" DeCenzo says. "He's the rational one of the group. He doesn't always say the nicest things in the world, but he says what's on his mind and what's on the audience's mind, and I think people really appreciate that."

DeCenzo says he can relate to Demetri's high-school-survivalist attitude. "I'm a nerd just like Demetri, and I was never the most popular person growing up," he says. "I had my set group of friends and that was all I needed. So when it comes to being an awkward teenager with little to no friends, I can certainly empathize. I'm not as sarcastic and don't have quite the dry wit that Demetri does, but I do try to pull from my own personal life for the character, and I think that's what makes him so natural to play." Eventually, his character does take up karate—a reaction to continual harassment from his former best friend Hawk— but his inclination toward self-preservation never entirely goes away.

No holistic picture of modern-day bullying is complete without giving attention to online harassment and cyberbullying, and Cobra Kai features plenty of each. In season one, Aisha is continually harassed by anonymous kids using fake social media accounts. In season four, Kenny, a new kid in town, is catfished by Daniel's son, Anthony LaRusso. And while online bullying is a very real danger in the lives of today's teens, it also serves as another reminder of just how much has changed since Johnny was in high school. "It's nice to have Johnny, who has his own views and can criticize that generation and say, 'no, no, no, you guys are doing it all wrong,'" Schlossberg says. "One of the first questions we asked ourselves was, 'What would Johnny Lawrence think of bullying today?' He would think they are cowards hiding behind their computers. Pretending to be somebody else, or throwing a criticism from afar

DALLAS DUPREE YOUNG (KENNY)

What was it like joining the series in season four, once it was already a hit and the cast already had such chemistry?

Joining the series in season four was incredibly nerve-racking for me. With the relationships already established, I didn't know how I would fit in with adults, but the cast welcomed me with open arms.

In what ways do you relate to your character?
Kenny and I related to each other because of our athletic ability, the kindness of our hearts, and our maturity levels.

Kenny goes through a huge evolution in season four–what do you think is going through his mind at the end of the season?
I think Kenny was unleashing all of his built-in aggression at the end of the season on one person. He already struggled mentally with bullying and then being publicly humiliated by Robby was the final straw.

What was it like playing opposite Tanner Buchanan? What advice did he give, as someone who's been in the show since season one?
Playing alongside Tanner Buchanan was surreal for me. Growing up, I used to watch Tanner's work, and having the opportunity to act in the same series was unbelievable. The advice he gave me was to enjoy every second of your childhood and don't wish to grow up too fast. Another piece of advice was to focus on technique rather than going through the motions quickly in karate.

over the internet, is like the dorkiest concept to him."

Johnny says it best when Aisha explains her traumatic experiences with cyberbullying. "What a bunch of pussies," he says. "Back in my day, if you wanted to tease someone, you did it to their face. There was honor, respect. These geeks hiding behind their computers, what a bunch of spineless losers."

While no one would want to encounter bullies like Kyler, Hawk, or Tory in real life, the actors behind these roles say there's nothing more fun than portraying a bad guy. List, who was previously best known for her role as sweet but ditzy Emma Ross in the Disney series *Jessie* and its spin-off *Bunk'd,* says she's relished taking on a tougher character. "I love getting to play someone who's so shameless," she says. "What I love about Tory is that if she sees something that she doesn't think is right, she'll fight it immediately. It's so much fun to play someone who won't take shit from anyone. I didn't realize I would feel this, but it's almost a therapeutic release, because I don't get to do that in my own life. I've had to listen to what other people tell me to do for so long, especially growing up in show business—it's always like, 'This is what you have to do, this is what you have to say, this is how you have to say it'—and there are times in my life when I've wanted to call people out or tell them off, but I would never behave that way.

To play this female who just does not care is the best ever."

Tory is one of the two main female fighters in the Miyagi-verse, and she and Samantha LaRusso share credit for expanding the idea of who can be a karate kid and for bringing in a larger female fan base. It's a privilege neither of them takes lightly. "Girls need to see themselves represented in a space in order to know they belong there," List says. "Not that Tory is the best example, but I'm glad that young girls come up to me and say they started taking karate because of Tory or because of Sam. It's my favorite thing to hear because girls *should* be learning self-defense and how to fight and protect themselves. They should be in those spaces. It's about time."

> **"Girls need to see themselves represented in a space in order to know they belong there."**
> **—Peyton List**

In her own life, List says she's had no choice but to prove she can keep up with the guys around her, so she's glad to show younger girls that it's possible. "I have a twin brother, so I grew up very much being on the same level, playing the same sports, doing the same things—it's not that new to me," she says. "I mean, at some point fighting with my brother wasn't my favorite thing, but we shared a bunk bed and a bedroom, so I had to be able to fight him and take him down in order to establish my own space."

Mary Mouser, who plays Samantha LaRusso, says she could have used a character like Sam as inspiration when she was a kid. "I'm so grateful to have this role because this is a character I really would have attached myself to when I was younger," she says. "Samantha doesn't 'fight like a girl'—in fact, she has eight years' experience on most of the guy fighters, because she trained with her dad as a kid and knew Mr. Miyagi. Karate is her form of catharsis and her version of yoga. And that's so me. Like, as Mary, I hated exercise. I hated anything where I was told to get centered and calm. I'm so bad at it. But I've found that fighting does it for me—it feels so good to get it all out. I wish I had seen this character in my teens because I would have thought, 'Maybe I should go get myself into karate or kickboxing.' That was exactly what I needed." Today, Mouser fights in real life—even when she's not filming—and says plenty of female fans have also followed in Samantha's footsteps. "They tell me 'Hey, I got into karate

OONA O'BRIEN (DEVON)

What was it like joining the series in season four, once it was already a hit and the cast already had such chemistry?

Intimidating! As a superfan of the show and movies, I was incredibly excited to meet the cast; but it was my first professional acting job, and I was pretty new to karate, so I was also really nervous. I spent the entire season trying not to be starstruck or laugh during takes. But everyone was super friendly and curious. Mr.

Zabka, Xolo, and all the Eagle Fang crew were so welcoming and generous. Because of COVID, we were discouraged from hanging out too much offset, but I bonded quickly w Nate, Owen, Griffin, and Dallas: we would eat lunch together every day, set-school, go t crafty, and play frisbee during breaks. Everyone works really hard, but they're always up for having fun. And the energy shooting the All Valley scenes was crazy; everyone came to support and hype each other up. That's the great thing about this cast; they're alway there for you. It really felt like one big family.

In what ways do you relate to your character?

I'm more chill than Devon, but when it comes to sports, I can be pretty competitive. I ha to lose. Also, I can be impatient with laziness. I love extra credit. I raise my hand a lot in class. And I really do love math. I guess I'm more like her than I thought!

There are more women in the Miyagi-verse than there once were, but it's still relatively new to have female fighters. Why is it so important that viewers see your character?

Having any Asian representation is super important in combating stereotypes of Asians in the martial arts, but being an Asian female takes it a step further. Devon's fierce competitiveness really challenges the notion of Asian females as being meek and submissive. And Devon starts karate at an age when lots of girls abandon sports. She's not in it for the drama; she latches on to karate as an outlet for her own sense of accomplishment, to push herself. I love that about her, and I hope she inspires other gir to do the same.

because of Samantha' and it blows my mind. It's impressive to me that young women are seeing this character on screen and thinking, 'Yes, I can do that.'"

But it's not just the fighting that makes Sam an essential TV character, Mouser explains. It's the confidence. "I love seeing women in strong roles, obviously, but a lot of times when I'm watching them, they feel unattainable to me. I'm like, 'Well, I don't have the tools and access of that woman, so I can't do what she's doing,'" Mouser says. "But seeing what Samantha does with just who she is and what she has at her disposal, it's really empowering. She went from being the nerd in science class to being someone who was fearless and, especially in season four, someone who says 'I'm going to take the bull by the horns and settle this rivalry myself. I'm going to take on the generational debt.'"

Mouser, a few years older than her character, often uses her own life experience to inform how she approaches the role. "I can say to myself, 'Okay, I remember this moment and how big it felt, and this is how I wish I handled the situation—or this is how I handled the situation and how it affected me," she says. "Those feelings Samantha has, of not knowing where she belongs and wanting to find her place, but not wanting to be exactly who her parents want her to be—it's definitely something I can relate to. Samantha was trying to figure

SAM AND TORY'S FEMALE FIGHTER INSPIRATION

Samantha LaRusso and Tory Nichols may be two of the first female fighters in the Miyagi-verse (shout-out to Aisha Robinson, Devon Lee, and also Julie Pierce from *The Next Karate Kid*), but there are plenty of ass-kicking women who have paved the way for their success. Here's who the ladies look up to when they need to get amped for a fight.

RONDA ROUSEY: UFC and WWE star "Rowdy" Ronda Rousey got her start in martial arts—she was the first American woman to earn an Olympic medal in judo with her bronze at the 2008 Summer Olympics, and then began a career in MMA. She competed in—and won—the first women's fight in UFC history and was the first woman inducted into the UFC Hall of Fame.

LAILA ALI: Like Sam, Laila Ali knows something about following in the footsteps of a legendary father and fighter. The daughter of Muhammad Ali, Laila became a professional boxer in 1999 and fought until 2007. She won ten championships and was undefeated when she retired.

CHENG PEI PEI: Also known as the "Queen of Kung Fu," Cheng Pei Pei began starring in kung-fu films in the 1960s. Considered the first female action hero, she's skilled with a both a sword and a staff. Her most notable films are 1966's *Come Drink with Me* and 2000's *Crouching Tiger, Hidden Dragon*.

SANDRA SÁNCHEZ: The Spanish karate champion won the gold medal in the women's kata event at the 2020 Summer Olympics in Tokyo, and the gold medal in the individual kata event at the European Karate Championships for six years in a row. As if that's not impressive enough, she won thirty-five consecutive medals in the World Karate Federation's Karate 1-Premiere League between January 2014 and February 2020.

out who she wanted to be all on her own, and then realized 'Maybe I don't have all the answers. Maybe I don't know who I want to be, maybe there *are* things I can take from what my mom and dad have taught me and apply those things to my own life.' I've definitely been there."

One of Sam's dad's most helpful teachings? How to deal with a long-standing rival. While Sam and Tory each showcase the power of female fighters, their characters couldn't be more at odds. Yet even their rivalry is groundbreaking, Mouser says, because it's more complicated than most on-screen female feuds. "I don't think I realized how seriously everybody would take Samantha and Tory's rivalry, but it's a testament to the incredible writers on the show that what could have been a classic 'girl fight' is so much more," Mouser says. "No story or history between any two people, regardless of gender, is ever as superficial as it's made out to be, but women have historically been dealt a hand in the media where their conflicts are written off or simplified to just 'catfight.' I love that our show doesn't do that. It looks at all the aspects that inform Tory and Sam's relationship—their different backgrounds and upbringings and social classes, plus the fear of not fitting in and the insecurities of being a teenager—in addition to the 'boy drama.'"

No matter how much Tory and Sam seem to hate each other on-screen, behind the scenes Mouser and List have become great friends. "Peyton is honestly the sweetest person ever," Mouser says. "We'll go to karaoke nights together or text about funny memes, and then we get to completely obliterate each other on-screen, which is really awesome." And theirs isn't the only on-screen feud that has translated into a friendship off the clock. When on location in Atlanta, Maridueña, Bertrand, and Joe Seo, who plays their tormentor Kyler, share a house together and go rock climbing on their days off.

Bertrand is also close friends with Gianni DeCenzo, a relationship that both actors say has helped create the chemistry of one of *Cobra Kai's* most beloved on-again, off-again friendships: the Binary Brothers. "I think the best way to describe their relationship is that they're like Ross and Rachel of *Friends*, but instead of 'Will they or won't they?' it's 'Will they or won't they kick the crap out of each other?'" DeCenzo says. After all, long before Eli became Hawk, before he was chasing Demetri through the mall or breaking his arm at the arcade, the two were best friends watching *Harry Potter* films, having sleepovers, and going to computer camp. In season four, viewers are even treated to the pair's "Binary Bros Theme Song" music video, complete with costumes, techno music, and wireless keyboards. "One thing that is really cool about that friendship is how awesome Demetri is," Bertrand says. "He was there for Hawk through literally everything—he was there when he was getting picked on, he even stuck up for Eli when he was getting mocked by Johnny, and that's not an easy thing to do. I think their relationship is so well received because everyone wants a friend like Demetri. Someone who is nothing but supportive, someone who calls you out on your bullshit but will be there to help you work through it."

It's a real roller coaster of a relationship—the two have a falling out when Demetri quits Cobra Kai and leaves the dojo a bad Yelp review, sparking serious hostility (and physical violence) between the one-time pals—but it stays true, in many ways, to the ups and downs of any childhood friendship. "I think a lot of people can relate to the fact that, to Demetri, Eli will always be Eli. In fact, the only time he ever calls him Hawk is when he's putting him down or being sarcastic, like 'Yeah, okay, *Hawk*,'" DeCenzo says. "It sucked to watch that friendship fall apart, so it was great to see them come back together at the end of season three and kick ass together."

During the season three finale fight at the LaRusso house, Hawk sees Demetri getting beat up by two Cobra Kais, and something suddenly clicks. "Seeing how cruel [Doug] Rickenberger is to Demetri, holding him down and kicking his ass, and watching Kyler, Hawk's former bully, beat up Miguel . . . I think he just realized that Cobra Kai isn't what it used to be," Bertrand says. "He was slow in realizing that, because he's bad at sticking up for himself, but seeing Demetri getting hurt helped him finally snap out of it." Bertrand says he can empathize with his character's struggle to realize who his true friends are. "A big part of Eli's growth is figuring out who to surround himself with, which was really hard for me growing up. The way he gets picked on and ostracized for so long, and then finally finds confidence and spreads his wings, so to speak, I really relate to Eli in that sense." Eventually in season four, Demetri convinces Hawk to join Miyagi-Do in an especially touching moment between the old pair. "I know you think that mohawk defined who you are, but it didn't, not to me," Demetri

GET TO KNOW . . . THE BINARY BROTHERS

Demetri and Eli have had their ups and downs, but there's no denying that theirs is the deepest friendship amongst the *Cobra Kai* teens. After all, long before they were sporting mohawks, interested in girls, and kicking ass, the Binary Brothers were crying over Dobby's death and going to computer camp. The series creators say the idea for this friendship started with their own experiences. "We loved the idea of these friends who are math- and science-based friends. They were like the friends we had in high school, some of whom would really nerd out on stuff that was only socially acceptable within our groups—like taking pride in how many digits of pi you can recite," says Josh Heald. "When the viewer meets Demetri and Eli at the beginning of season one, Demetri is a gregarious kid but only in the small sphere of him and Eli. We wanted to play with the idea of what happens to a friendship like this when one of the kids starts doing something more socially popular, like when Hawk starts doing karate."

The duo's name comes from the ones and zeros of binary coding, and the creators say coming up with the creative "nerd details" of their friendship was especially rewarding. "The Binary Brothers are a representation of the nerdiest versions of ourselves, and the nerdiest sides of every writer in the writers' room," Jon Hurwitz says. "We are all nerds in different ways. That Cherry Pi shirt Demetri wears? I wore that in high school."

says. "Eli, Hawk, hell, call yourself Cornelius for all I care. None of that changes that you're my binary brother. Whether you're number one . . . or a zero."

No matter whether the two pals are thick as thieves or on the outs, the history and connection between Hawk and Demetri is palpable, and both actors agree it's because they're so close off-screen. Bertrand and DeCenzo have become tight in the years since filming first began, linking up for heart-to-heart conversations about the pressures of starring in a hit TV show or to simply play *Magic: The Gathering*. "In season four, we have serious scenes together, and Gianni is able to keep it really light in between takes and then switch back quickly to the heavy stuff, and I think that's because we talk about serious stuff all the time. We're very comfortable with each other," Bertrand says.

As DeCenzo puts it: "Shout-out to Jacob. He's my real-life binary brother."

05
LARUSSO
AUTO GROUP

"KICKING THE COMPETITION"

*I*n the Miyagi-verse, a character's ride can tell you many things: how they feel about themselves, who they aspire to be, and, naturally, what they can afford. And that's been the case ever since the opening scene of the original *Karate Kid* film, when Daniel and his mother, Lucille, are seen driving cross-country in a beat-up station wagon that Daniel repeatedly has to push-start to get moving. For most of the first movie, Daniel's only wheels are his Mongoose Two/Four bicycle. Johnny, on the other hand, drives a 1983 Avanti convertible, the epitome of *cool* at the time. As the movie progresses, Daniel becomes obsessed with the idea of getting his own car. "He's riding this bicycle while the cool rich kids have motorbikes and cars," Hayden Schlossberg says. "Then, when he goes to Mr. Miyagi's place, he's looking at the cars, which are a symbol of independence and the idea that you're not a kid anymore. The first step toward adulthood is learning how to drive, and that was important to the movie."

When *Cobra Kai*'s creators were envisioning where Daniel would be working thirty years after the original movie, they immediately liked the idea of putting him at the helm of a car dealership. "We asked ourselves, if Johnny is down and out, in what way would Daniel be successful?" Schlossberg says. "Considering one of his biggest interests in the films was cars, we thought that would be a fun way for him to have 'made it.' We figured maybe Mr. Miyagi, through his teachings, taught him to cut through all the slimy car salesman stuff to be someone who is successful in a justifiable way."

Enter the LaRusso Auto Group. Owned by Daniel and Amanda—with Daniel's cousin Louie LaRusso Jr. (played by Bret Ernst) and their friend Anoush Norouzi (played by Dan Ahdoot) working sales—the dealership serves as a marker of the family's success while also revealing some of Daniel's blind spots. "Daniel has the best of intentions pretty much all the time, but he doesn't necessarily realize the ways he's being perceived or the way—with the 'chopping prices' and the bonsais and the 'kicking the competition'—it might appear that he's misutilizing some of Mr. Miyagi's lessons," Jon Hurwitz

says. This notion that Daniel doesn't always see himself clearly is a theme that continues throughout the show's seasons, but is showcased most clearly in his TV commercials and billboards. In one particular display of comic cheesiness, Daniel is shown literally karate chopping car prices on-screen, complete with glass-shattering sound effects as the prices drop by a few thousand dollars.

"There's an element of cheesiness there that is tied to the spirit of the show that we're making, so there's a comedic bent to it as well," Hurwitz notes. The person most put off by the corny advertising? Johnny Lawrence. Thirty years later, he's still reminded on a regular basis of the crane kick that ended his high school reign. In fact, it's only five minutes into the first episode when Johnny spots a new billboard. "Not another one," he groans.

"We wanted Daniel to still be a thorn in Johnny's side, but not a person in his actual life," Hurwitz says of the setup for the series. "If you live in the Valley and LaRusso owns all these car dealerships, then you can't help but hear the radio commercials and see the billboards. We felt it was an organic way to make Daniel still top of mind for Johnny, even though all these years have passed."

Macchio admits that, at least at first, he wasn't totally sold on the idea of Daniel as a car dealer. "In the early pitch, the guys were like, 'He's a car salesman,' and I was like 'Really?' but I knew I had to hear them out," he says. "I wanted to make sure we were honest to where LaRusso would be at this point. I understand the comedy in Johnny Lawrence seeing this guy on television or on a billboard kicking the competition—it's just his worst nightmare—but would Daniel LaRusso have landed there in my eyes? I'm not sure I would have written it that way, but I understood why it supported this angle of storytelling. The guys and I always discussed that the dealership would be the starting point, but the show would evolve to other places. So maybe Daniel did have the one crane kick that he carried with him for twenty years, like the guy who scores the touchdown in the Texas high school football league and becomes famous in the town." Macchio says one of his earliest discussions with the creators centered around the LaRusso Auto Group commercial when viewers see Daniel for the first time. "I think if it were up to Jon, Josh, and Hayden, Daniel would have been wearing the white T-shirt and the headband on TV," he says. "But I was very specific about, let's negotiate how we're going to bring him into the show. It's all been extraordinarily collaborative—I give notes and we always talk through stuff, but at the end of the day they get the tiebreaker, because they are driving the ship and it's too precious to me. Sometimes I have to step back and defer to them for the aerial view."

If the success of LaRusso Auto Group serves in some part to showcase Daniel's blind spots, it's also a testament to the strength of Daniel and Amanda's relationship. Not every husband and wife could withstand doubling as coworkers. "They built a business together—a very successful business. It shows there is a lot of trust with them," Courtney Henggeler, who plays Amanda, says. "There's so much familiarity, which you *need* in a marriage. Daniel's life is going off the rails in a lot of ways. He's got to have one thing that's stable in his life, and hopefully that's me."

Creating a car dealership also gave the creators a perfect opportunity to

ANOUSH AND LOUIE'S SALES TIPS

LOUIE

You wanna know how to sell cars? Well, lucky for you, my cousin is the top auto dealer in the Valley, and I'm his most experienced salesman. And Anoush here is okay, too.

ANOUSH

I've worked here longer than you.

LOUIE

First thing, you gotta let people know you're in charge. Don't ask customers what they want—tell them.

ANOUSH

Don't do that.

LOUIE

Dealerships can be intense. It's cool to let off steam sometimes— play a prank on the new guy. He'll love it!

ANOUSH

Try to avoid upsetting your boss's karate rivals. There might be a lot of them, though. And it feels like he's always adding new ones.

LOUIE

You don't let anyone diss your dealership, okay? Someone draws a dick on your billboard, you take care of it like a man.

ANOUSH

Because that worked out so well for you.

LOUIE

Come on, man, why you gotta bring that up?

remind viewers that this fictional show takes place in a real-life city. "When we were kids, the Valley might as well have been Gotham City or Metropolis, or Hill Valley in *Back to the Future*," Schlossberg says. "It was this microcosm of the world with a good, rich part of town, and a bad side of tracks. And we utilize that, but there are some fun things about basing this show in a real place. If you've ever lived in Southern California, you know cars are such an important part of life there, and you'll see some very similar local car commercials. It's true to life."

"They built a business together—a very successful business. It shows there is a lot of trust with them. There's so much familiarity, which you *need* in a marriage. Daniel's life is going off the rails in a lot of ways. He's got to have one thing that's stable in his life, and hopefully that's me." —Courtney Henggeler (Amanda LaRusso)

When conceiving of Daniel's business rival, Tom Cole, owner of the dealership Cole's on Van Nuys, the creators originally wanted to use the name of a real-life successful Valley auto dealer. "If you drive up and down Van Nuys Boulevard in the Valley, it's like the picture of Valley success. Whoever Keyes is, that guy is probably doing pretty well because Keyes on Van Nuys—well, there's a Keyes everything. Keyes Honda, Keyes BMW, Keyes Mercedes," Josh Heald says. Before season one, *Cobra Kai* production reached out to the real-life Keyes family in hopes that they could use the name to introduce a character named Tom Keyes, a professional nemesis who would be a fictionalized version of the real-life car dealer. "We wanted to introduce the idea that there is this family who owns car sales in the Valley and LaRusso has become successful enough and powerful enough to also have a seat at that table, and we thought it would be a fun way to show what the Valley really is." Unfortunately, the Keyes group expressed no interest in being featured, so the entirely fictionalized Tom Cole was devised instead.

While the dealership is a symbol of Daniel's good fortune—as is the Audi S7 he drives to work each morning—cars tell a clear story of status on Johnny's

side as well. He has a number of different vehicles throughout the series' first four seasons, starting with the Pontiac Firebird—a supercool car . . . in 1991. "It's clear when the audience meets Johnny that he's clinging to the past based on the car he's driving," Schlossberg says. When the Firebird gets torched by Louie LaRusso, Daniel lets Johnny choose a new ride from his lot, and he goes with a red Dodge Challenger. The name itself is symbolic—Johnny and the new Cobra Kai seem to challenge Daniel and the current Valley status quo—and as the updated Cobra Kai dojo gains success, the Challenger gets its own reinvention. At the beginning of season two, Johnny uses his newfound earnings to get the car sprayed black with yellow decals, adding a new Cobra Kai vanity plate and a snake-shaped gear shift. At the end of season two, after Kreese has taken control of Cobra Kai and Miguel is admitted to the hospital, Johnny ditches the Challenger at the beach—it's a moment that illustrates just how defeated Johnny is feeling as he leaves Cobra Kai behind. In season three, he starts driving a Dodge Caravan. It's a minivan that's a bit more practical, if somewhat tired—not unlike Johnny himself at that point. And just as Johnny gains a new edge with the advent of Eagle Fang, so too does the Caravan. In season four, the car has been spray-painted with an eagle face (complete with fangs,

of course) and bright-red talons. The minivan reflects its driver: a little more responsible, but still badass.

Given the significance that cars hold for both Daniel and Johnny, it should come as no surprise that, as different as the two men may seem, it's during a test drive in season one that viewers get the first hint the characters may be more similar than they realize. When Johnny is at LaRusso Auto Group picking out the Firebird replacement, he and Daniel take a test drive in the Challenger—finding common ground as they nod along to REO Speedwagon's "Take It on the Run" and reminisce about the old days in an episode aptly titled "Different but Same." During the drive, they stop for a visit to the Reseda apartment complex where Daniel lived in *The Karate Kid*, and it's there that Johnny reveals he didn't exactly have it made in high school. While sharing a drink at a bar, the two men finally compare notes on their upbringings.

In season three, another shared car ride between Daniel and Johnny—this time to find Robby, who's on the run after the big high school fight—has the two playing a spoken version of "good cop, bad cop," a rapport that reemerges when they team up as "Miyagi-Fang" senseis in season four. But why is Daniel so invested in finding Robby? Because he wants to do for another kid in need what Mr. Miyagi did for him. In fact, Daniel does a lot of bonding with the younger generation throughout *Cobra Kai*. First, he connects with Robby after

JOHNNY LAWRENCE'S ROAD-TRIP PLAYLIST

Nothing's better than cruising down Ventura Boulevard, windows down, music blaring. But none of that boyband crap. Next time you're tempted to blast whatever TikTok sensation is masquerading as a singer these days, try queueing up these fast-rockin' Johnny-approved tracks instead.

A

Poison, "Nothin' but a Good Time"

Ratt, "Lay It Down"

Twisted Sister, "We're Not Gonna Take It"

REO Speedwagon, "Take It on the Run"

Queen, "I Want It All"

AC/DC, "Back in Black"

Whitesnake, "Here I Go Again"

Ratt, "Round and Round"

Twisted Sister, "I Wanna Rock"

Motley Crüe, "Kickstart My Heart"

B

- Guns N' Roses, "Welcome to the Jungle"
- Scorpions, "Rock You Like a Hurricane"
- Metallica, "Seek & Destroy"
- AC/DC, "You Shook Me All Night Long"
- Styx, "Too Much Time on My Hands"
- Van Halen, "Jump"
- Joan Jett, "I Love Rock 'n' Roll"
- Bon Jovi, "Wanted Dead or Alive"
-
-
-

EASTER EGGS

Cobra Kai includes many Easter-egg references to the original movies. Here are just a few—how many did you spot?

SEASON ONE, EPISODE ONE, "ACE DEGENERATE"
The episode title is a reference to what Johnny's friends call him at the beginning of *The Karate Kid*—he's the "ace degenerate."

SEASON ONE, EPISODE THREE, "ESQUELETO"
Miguel wears a skeleton costume similar to the one Johnny wore to the Halloween dance in *The Karate Kid*.

SEASON ONE, EPISODE SEVEN, "ALL VALLEY"
Miguel and Sam's Golf N' Stuff montage is almost a shot-for-shot re-creation of Daniel and Ali's date in *The Karate Kid*.

SEASON TWO, EPISODE FIVE, "ALL IN"
The song "No Shelter" plays as Demetri runs away from the Cobra Kais—the same song playing as Johnny chases Daniel in *The Karate Kid*.

SEASON TWO, EPISODE SIX, "TAKE A RIGHT"
The episode title is a reference to Tommy's line in *The Karate Kid*—"Take a right, check it out!"

SEASON TWO, EPISODE SEVEN, "LULL"
The freezer Daniel takes his students to contains meat branded with the name "Fernandez Meats." This is a reference to Freddy Fernandez, who Daniel met when he arrived at his new apartment complex at the beginning of *The Karate Kid*.

SEASON THREE, EPISODE ONE, "AFTERMATH"

Kreese now has a cardboard cutout of himself in the dojo—similar to the one in *The Karate Kid Part III*.

SEASON THREE, EPISODE FIVE, "MIYAGI-DO"

If you look closely in Chozen's dojo, you'll see a relic from *The Karate Kid* cartoon.

SEASON THREE, EPISODE TEN, "DECEMBER 19"

This episode takes place on December 19, the date of the All Valley Tournament in *The Karate Kid*.

SEASON FOUR, EPISODE ONE, "LET'S BEGIN"

The bottle of wine that Terry Silver kicks is from "Kamen Estates"—the vineyard belonging to Robert Mark Kamen, who wrote *The Karate Kid* movies.

SEASON FOUR, EPISODE FIVE, "MATCH POINT"

When Demetri is digging up info on Terry Silver, he finds a reference to "a toxic waste scandal in Borneo in the '80s." In *The Karate Kid Part III*, Silver is shown ordering his company to dump toxic waste in Borneo.

SEASON FOUR, EPISODE TEN, "THE RISE"

When Miguel doesn't return to the mat after his injury, the announcer declares, "Miguel Diaz is NOT gonna fight!" This is an homage to the scene from *The Karate Kid*, when, as Daniel returns to the mat, the announcer yells "Daniel LaRusso is gonna fight!"

DANIEL: "Your stepdad was an asshole, huh? Back in the day I just figured you were living the life, you know? Fancy cars, motorbikes . . ."

JOHNNY: "It had its moments. Then I'd come home and pretty much get bullied every day. That's why I joined Cobra Kai. Kreese gave me more attention than I ever got at home. The guy was more than a sensei to me. He was basically a father. Anyway, you wouldn't understand."

DANIEL: "My dad died when I was eight. Mr. Miyagi was like a father to me. It's crazy, man. Both finding karate role models."

he starts working at the car dealership, and in season four he establishes an unexpected connection with Miguel. The two have their first real conversation while sitting in the '47 Ford, and in season four, Daniel teaches Miguel to drive. It's a milestone moment for any teenager, and the fact that it's shared between Daniel and Miguel is a sore spot for Johnny, who resents the pair's increasing closeness. "Daniel brings a bit of fresh perspective to Miguel," Xolo Maridueña says of that relationship. "He's a little bit more compassionate with Miguel than Johnny is, but we see that it makes Johnny jealous—these guys can never just have nice things—so that relationship proves to be a little more difficult than

Miguel or Daniel anticipated. But I think the compassion is what Miguel likes about Daniel. Not to mention, people are like, 'Hey, you guys kind of look similar,' so that's funny."

The influence of cars, and the LaRusso Auto Group specifically, reverberates all the way to the end of season four, when cameras flash to what appears to be a forthcoming unexpected partnership: Daniel and Chozen Toguchi, the villain from *The Karate Kid II*. Viewers are first reintroduced to Chozen in season three, when Daniel travels to Japan for a business trip. Doyona International, a fictional importer of Japanese cars, threatens to pull its contract with LaRusso Auto Group, which would be a devastating blow to the business, so Daniel flies overseas to try and save the company. After his business meeting, Daniel goes to Okinawa in an attempt to reconnect with Mr. Miyagi's memory, and there he bumps into Kumiko, and later, Chozen. Much of the episode was filmed in Okinawa and for Macchio, getting to travel to what he calls "sacred ground" in the Karate Kid universe was powerful. "It reminded me of when I was in Hawaii filming *Karate Kid Part II*, but this time, I was actually in the land of Miyagi, and it was breathtaking," Macchio said in a video he posted on Twitter. "It's been very special to be here. . . . It's about as close as I could get to having Pat Morita in our show, and the spirit of Miyagi living on. So, it was important to me, and to production."

While the indoor scenes of the Okinawa-based episodes were filmed

CHOZEN TOGUCHI

DOJO: Miyagi-Do

ALLY: Daniel LaRusso

NEMESES: Daniel LaRusso (former), Mr. Miyagi (former),

Terry Silver

CHARACTER PHILOSOPHY: "We fight when the time is right."

LOVE INTEREST: Kumiko

FAMILY: Sato Toguchi (uncle)

THE PRESSURE POINTS TECHNIQUE

In season three, Daniel travels to Okinawa, Japan, and reconnects with Chozen Toguchi, his *Karate Kid II* nemesis. The two men—basically "karate cousins," Daniel points out, because their senseis shared the same sensei—end up sparring after Daniel makes the claim that Mr. Miyagi taught him "everything he knew." In order to prove that Daniel doesn't know *everything*, Chozen incapacitates him with the "pressure points technique," a secret Miyagi method that renders an opponent's limbs temporarily paralyzed. "If an enemy insists on war, you take away his ability to wage it," Chozen explains. As the episode progresses, Chozen teaches Daniel the ancient technique, which Miyagi apparently thought was too dangerous to teach Daniel back in the day.

The idea for the pressure points technique came from Robert Mark Kamen, writer of the original *Karate Kid* films, who was a dedicated karate student himself. After the first season of *Cobra Kai*, Kamen connected with series creators Josh Heald, Jon Hurwitz, and Hayden Schlossberg—they have since all become close friends. "We talk with him about some of the karate-specific stuff before each season," Schlossberg says. "He taught us about the concept of scrolls that show karate moves, which is a real piece of Okinawan folklore and was featured in season three, and in that conversation he also mentioned the idea of using the pressure points as a technique to disarm your opponent." The creators thought it sounded dangerous but intriguing. "We all remember the crane kick in the original movie, so the three of us were wondering, 'Could there be other secrets that Mr. Miyagi didn't tell Daniel about? Or that we, the viewer, didn't know about?'" Schlossberg says. This idea of using pressure points, they realized, was a perfect fit. And while Miyagi's version of a pressure points technique isn't exactly a real-life karate method, Schlossberg notes that "It's based on something real, we just gave it a bit of a Hollywood twist."

in Atlanta, the outdoor scenes with Daniel and Chozen were shot during a whirlwind two-day trip to Japan that included Schlossberg, Macchio, Yuji Okumoto, who plays Chozen, and a skeleton crew. "The first day, our scouting day, was beautiful weather, but the second day, our shooting day, the weather was torrential rain and wind," Schlossberg says. "By the time we started shooting the scene on the mountain where Ralph and Yuji bow to each other, the rain let up a little bit, but if you watch that episode you can see, behind Ralph, that the wind is blowing the leaves like crazy. And getting Ralph's hair to stay put and not look like Doc Brown in *Back to the Future* was a challenge, but it ended up working out. Those scenes ended up in the trailer for the season and give an authenticity to the franchise that the original movies didn't necessarily have."

During those episodes, Daniel learns that Chozen has turned his life around since they last saw one another and has taken over as sensei of Miyagi-Do in Okinawa. Daniel also learns of some surprisingly aggressive Miyagi-Do moves, including the pressure points technique, which serves to numb an opponent's limbs. Chozen trains Daniel in the technique, and in the third season finale, Daniel uses it to temporarily paralyze Kreese during a brutal fight between the two at the Cobra Kai dojo. Ultimately, the trip to Okinawa proves to be redeeming on multiple fronts: it's responsible for keeping LaRusso Auto Group in business (after Daniel reunites with Yuni, the woman whose life he saved when she was just a girl in *Karate Kid II*, she helps him keep Doyona's business—turns out she now works as the company's senior vice president of sales), and it equips Daniel with new Miyagi-Do techniques to employ against the enemy.

The LaRusso Auto Group may have been created, at least in part, as a plot device—a way to pit Daniel against Johnny and frame Daniel's sometimes cheesy success in the world of the Valley—but it's ultimately a starting point for many of the series' most impactful relationships. Macchio himself, though skeptical at first, came around to appreciating the creators' motives. "In the end, it helps us see the center of who Daniel LaRusso is—the good intentions, even through his failures and missteps," Macchio says. "To play it safe wouldn't have been as entertaining."

06
GOLF N' STUFF

"ALL THE BABES WANT TO DATE A COBRA KAI"

First dates. Dances. Friday nights at the drive-in. They're the defining moments in any teenager's life, and the karate kids of the Valley are no different. These slice-of-life experiences are just as critical to the Miyagi-verse as fighting, and the coming-of-age action in *Cobra Kai* goes down at the same place it did thirty years before: Golf N' Stuff Family Fun Center, a local hangout with rides, an arcade, and, of course, mini golf. With its nostalgic decor, Golf N' Stuff is the one spot in the Miyagi-verse where time seems to have stood still. "It was fun to make Golf N' Stuff a place where kids today are still gathering, and because we have a TV series, we were able to incorporate it in other ways, like finding out that a character like [Miyagi-Do student] Chris is working there and seeing that the Cobra Kais are going to torment the Miyagi-Dos there," Jon Hurwitz says.

While Golf N' Stuff is a real franchise—there are two locations in California and one in Arizona—the *Cobra Kai* Golf N' Stuff scenes are shot on location at Fun Spot America in Atlanta (the team used special visual effects to get the spinning Golf N' Stuff sign from the original film into the exterior Georgia shots). That same filming location was used for season two's Valley Fest, as well as all of Kreese's Vietnam flashback scenes. And it's one of the few recurring locations in the series that's not a set built for the show. (Other on-location settings include the high school—production built a West Valley set for seasons three and four, but the high school scenes in the first two seasons were filmed at Atlanta Technical College; the strip-mall that houses the Cobra Kai dojo, though a couple of scenes—when Moon breaks up with Hawk, and when Kreese and Daniel crash through the window—were shot on a production-built stage; and the All Valley Tournament, which has been filmed at two separate high schools.) However, Golf N' Stuff isn't the only place where the teens in the series hang out in their free time, and in each of these locations,

DEMETRI'S DATING TIPS

You may be asking yourself, how did that big ol' geek Demetri land a hottie like Yasmine? Witchcraft? Bribery? Blackmail? Fear not, my friends, for I am about to share my considerable wisdom. Here's how to date the most popular girl in school:

1. Wait for her to become less popular—The basic economic law of supply and demand applies perfectly to the high school dating ecosystem. If you're competing with every guy in school for her attention, you're shit outta luck. But! Wait for her to drop down the pecking order—via, say, a vicious front wedgie, just for example—and pretty soon you'll be her only option!

2. Make yourself as pathetic as possible—Counterintuitive? Yes. Effective? Eventually! What starts as pity can often grow into true love. So go ahead, let her feel sorry for you! Note: serious potential to backfire.

3. Just be yourself—"What?" I hear you cry. "The same self that gets shoved into lockers and has no hope of getting laid before college, or even during college?" Yes, because the right girl for you is the one who appreciates you, dorkiness and all. Yasmine loves when I talk nerdy—I even got her to watch Star Wars with me (first trilogy only, original cut—Han shot first). Seriously, you do you. But learning a bit of karate won't hurt your chances.

the creators made an effort to incorporate nostalgia, reminding viewers of the show's connection to its movie predecessor and the universality of the teenage experience. "Whether it's the roller rink or the drive-in movie theater, we enjoyed finding different spots that felt sort of timeless and putting our teenagers there," Hurwitz says.

Though many of these locations are hosts to a teeny bit of teenage romance—the roller rink was the site of Samantha and Robby's *Pretty in Pink*–themed '80s-night outing—when it comes to first dates and first kisses in the Miyagi-verse, Golf N' Stuff is the old standby. In the original film, it's where Daniel LaRusso and Ali Mills have their first date; and in the *Cobra Kai* season one episode "All Valley," it's where Miguel takes Samantha. Miguel and Samantha's first date is almost identical, shot for shot, to Daniel and Ali's from the movie: the mini golf, the photo booth, even the Super Chexx hockey arcade game that the couples play while making eyes at one another. Superfans might even notice that the song playing in the background during Sam and Miguel's date, "Young Hearts" by Commuter, also plays during a Golf N' Stuff scene toward the end of *The Karate Kid*.

In season one, Johnny reveals that he, too, had his first date with Ali at Golf N' Stuff. After meeting during a 1982 showing of *Rocky III*, they shared their first kiss on the Ferris wheel. Though that original date was never caught on-screen, Johnny and Ali reconnect in the penultimate episode of season three, meeting for lunch and then going to—where else?—Golf N' Stuff, where they play air hockey, skee ball, and ride the Ferris wheel. The song playing in the background of this Golf N' Stuff outing, "Feel the Night" by Baxter Robertson, is also the name of the episode, and it's the same song playing in the background of Daniel and Ali's first date in *The Karate Kid*. Easter eggs, while never a conscious effort, come naturally to the show's creators. "There's always a way to draw an analogy to *The Karate Kid*," Hayden Schlossberg says. "We don't look for how can we add something in, but we're working with characters from that world, and oftentimes these are their memories. But there are still things we haven't done—you haven't seen Daniel catch a fly with his chopsticks—because the opportunity hasn't naturally presented itself."

Getting Elisabeth Shue to reprise her *Karate Kid* role of Ali Mills on *Cobra*

Kai was a longtime goal of the show creators . . . and a longtime dream of the series' fans. Ali's character looms large throughout the series—she's the initial cause of Daniel and Johnny's rivalry (she dated Johnny in high school, and after they broke up, Daniel showed up and stole her heart), and she's often shown in flashbacks or invoked by the men when waxing nostalgic about their high school days or rehashing the beginning of their feud. She's also the character who, albeit unknowingly, brings Johnny into the twenty-first century. He can't resist Facebook once Daniel tells him Ali can be found there, now named Ali Mills Schwarber and working as a doctor in Colorado. The showrunners say that many of Johnny's social media mishaps and faux pas were crafted, at least in part, to pave the way for a Johnny-Ali reunion. "We needed him to be able to connect with Ali, and that had to be through social media. It's the only thing that made sense and wasn't going to make her magically fall out of the heavens," Josh Heald says. "So it was a little bit of a drip, drip, drip to get him there. First, let's see him on a computer, then let's get him a smartphone, then let's put Facebook on that smartphone."

By the time production was ramping up for season three, the creators knew the time was right for Ali's return. First of all, the fans were clamoring for an Elisabeth Shue appearance, both on social media and in the creators' own lives. "My wife, from day one, was like 'When is Ali coming back?'" Hurwitz says. "And pretty much every guy we knew who had a crush on Elisabeth Shue, which was literally every guy we knew, was asking 'When is she coming back?' It wasn't a minor thing. It was everyone who had ever heard of the show wanted her back." But also, it was becoming clear that the show's time on YouTube Red could be ending. "During production on season three we started to see the writing on the wall with YouTube, so it was no surprise to us when they came and said, 'We're going to stop making original programming,'" Hurwitz says. "So, even though every season we're determined to make a show we think is undeniably great and people will enjoy, I remember while putting together season three we were like, 'Let's kick some ass here. Let's make sure, when we're trying to get Ali—Elisabeth Shue—on the show, that we don't take no for an answer, and that we deliver everything the fans will love.'"

Courtney Henggeler, who plays Amanda LaRusso, says filming alongside

JOHNNY'S QUINTESSENTIAL '80S GEAR

The '80s are back, baby! (Though some might say they never went out of style.) Perfect your killer '80s look with these Johnny Lawrence wardrobe staples.

PLAID SHIRT: They worked for me in high school, so why wouldn't they work for me now? If it ain't broke, you know? Wear over a T-shirt or baseball tee, no exceptions.

CONCERT TEES: There's no better way to pledge your allegiance to the greatest decade than with an authentic concert T-shirt. Be it Whitesnake, Metallica, Scorpions, Styx, AC/DC, Poison, Ratt, Zebra, or Red Hot Chili Peppers, rocking a killer concert tee tells the world you know how to party.

LEVI'S: Only an idiot would pay a shit ton for fancy denim that already has holes in it. Levi's are classics for a reason. Wear them when you're expecting a fight, and they'll be "distressed" in no time.

RED VINYL JACKET AND HEADBAND: Chicks dig a bad boy, and you don't need to be in full karate gear to show that you can take someone out with one swift kick. Nothing says "I'm gonna kick your ass and look good doing it" quite like a headband and vinyl bomber. Anyone who thinks headbands should be saved for the mat never had to face down a fight in the middle of a parking lot . . . or a bar . . . or a warehouse.

FRANK HELMER

What goes into creating Johnny's wardrobe? What is the key to his style?
Johnny's essential style is an effortless, easy, worn-in authentic cool influenced by '80s Southern California surf-and-skate culture. He basically still dresses more or less like he did in high school when he was at the height of his coolness.

For the concert tees specifically, what makes the perfect vintage '80s tee?
I choose only tees from bands that Johnny Lawrence would be a fan of and I source vintage original and replica tees from tours that came through Southern California. We imagine that he got the tees he wears at the concerts he attended in the '80s and '90s and they are perfectly faded, worn, and loved.

What is it, in Johnny's view, that makes a concert tee so cool?
The concert tee to Johnny represents the good times and great music that is the soundtrack to his life (and usually the show). His musical taste hasn't changed at all over the years and the memories of the concerts are important parts of his character.

Macchio, Zabka, and Shue has been a highlight of her time on the series. After their Golf N' Stuff outing, Johnny and Ali head to Encino Oaks Country Club for the annual Christmas party, where they bump into Daniel and Amanda. The foursome end up spending the evening together. "That was probably the most surreal day of filming for me, being with all three of them," says Henggeler, who notes that even the actors themselves waxed nostalgic. It was as though they were teenagers again, just catching up at the mall, rather than grown actors with children of their own. "They have all this history. They went through this journey together thirty years ago, and I'm like 'Hi, you're cute! I love your hair!' It was a very weird but very magical day."

The scene at the country club is the first time the characters of Amanda and Ali meet, and Henggeler notes it would have been easy for the writers to play up tension or jealousy between Daniel's wife and his ex. Luckily, she says, the story didn't take that turn. "The writers could have made them 'catty women' and it could have been funny, but it would have been the obvious approach, and I don't think that's Amanda and Ali's story," Henggeler says. What the writers created instead was a knowing interaction between two women who connect over their shared eyeroll at the series' leading men. "Our brilliant

JOHNNY TAKES A STAB AT
SOCIAL MEDIA #HASHBROWNS
SEND IT TO THE INTERNET!

AND THEN IN 1992, IRON EAGLE 3 CAME OUT. YOU KNOW WHAT? I DON'T CARE WHAT THE CRITICS SAY, I THOUGHT IT WAS PRETTY GOOD. NOT AS GOOD AS IRON EAGLE 1 AND IRON EAGLE 2, BUT HEY, WHAT MOVIE IS? I THINK WAYNE'S WORLD WAS THAT YEAR TOO. THAT ONE WAS OKAY. THOSE NERDS HAD GREAT TASTE IN MUSIC, AND THE CHICK WAS HOT. WHAT WAS SHE DOING WITH HIM? HOW COME THE HOT CHICKS GO FOR THE LOSERS IN THESE MOVIES? ANYWAY, OTHER THAN THAT 1992 WAS A PRETTY QUIET YEAR. GOT FIRED AGAIN, BUT WHAT THE HELL DO THEY KNOW? I DIDN'T LIKE CONSTRUCTION ANYWAY. THEY ALL SPEAK SPANISH AND I'M PRETTY SURE THEY WERE MAKING FUN OF ME SOMETIMES. DO YOU KNOW WHAT A "GRINGO" IS? I STARTED LEARNING A LITTLE BIT OF SPANISH FROM MIGUEL AND HIS FAMILY. I KNOW "HOLA", "PLANTAIN", "TACO" AND "DINERO." PRETTY GOOD, HUH? WHERE WAS I? OH, RIGHT, 1993. THERE WAS THAT DINOSAUR MOVIE. PRETTY GOOD FOR THE NINETIES. I MEAN, NOT ANYWHERE NEAR WHAT WE HAD BACK IN THE DAY. REMEMBER PREDATOR? THAT MOVIE WAS BADASS! THIS DINOSAUR THING WAS PRETTY COOL BUT TOO MUCH SCIENCEY STUFF FOR ME. I GUESS YOU PROBABLY LIKED THAT THOUGH, RIGHT? I MEAN, YOU'RE A DOCTOR NOW. I COULD NEVER BE A DOCTOR. NOT AFTER THAT INCIDENT AT COMMUNITY COLLEGE (I TALKED ABOUT THAT A COUPLE PARAGRAPHS AGO, DOES FACEBOOK LET YOU GO BACK AND REREAD?) STILL THINK THEY OVERREACTED. ALL THE GREAT SCIENTISTS SET THINGS ON FIRE, RIGHT? LIKE EINSTEIN OR WHOEVER. ANYWAY, 1993. DUTCH GOT ARRESTED. THAT ONE WAS PRETTY STUPID. I WAS DRUNK FOR MOST OF IT, BUT I'M PRETTY SURE HE

HOTWIRED A GOLF CART FROM THE COUNTRY CLUB. I LOOKED UP FROM THE BAR AND DUTCH IS DRIVING THIS THING AT HIGH SPEED, OR I GUESS AS HIGH AS SOMETHING LIKE THAT CAN GO, AND CRASHES IT INTO THE POOL! THEY HAD TO BRING A CRANE IN TO GET IT OUT. HE DID SOME TIME BUT IT WAS WORTH IT! ANYWAY, I DON'T THINK I'VE BEEN BACK TO THE COUNTRY CLUB SINCE THEN. SID WON'T LET THEM BAN ME BUT THOSE GUYS ARE ALL UPTIGHT, AND THEY ONLY SERVE FOREIGN BEER. IT'S OFFENSIVE. WE WON TWO WORLD WARS DRINKING AMERICAN BEER. WHAT THE HELL HAS BELGIUM EVER DONE EXCEPT GET INVADED? WHO WANTS TO DRINK THAT SHIT? I THINK I GOT OFF TOPIC AGAIN. LET'S GET BACK TO THE MID-NINETIES. 1994 WAS A SLOW YEAR. THE NINETIES SUCKED, MAN. YOU TURNED ON THE RADIO AND IT WAS JUST CRAP. WHO WRITES A SONG ABOUT BEING A LOSER? AND ALL THOSE GRUNGEY TYPES WITH THE FLANNEL. LET ME TELL YOU MUSIC IS SUPPOSED TO BE ABOUT BEING BADASS AND AWESOME, NOT ABOUT WANTING TO KILL YOURSELF. THAT SHIT CAN'T BE GOOD FOR KIDS TO HEAR, RIGHT? LOOK AT ME, WORRYING ABOUT WHAT THE KIDS ARE HEARING. I GUESS BEING A PARENT CHANGES YOU. NOT THAT I'M ALL THAT GREAT OF A PARENT. WELL, MIGUEL SEEMS TO LIKE ME OKAY. ROBBY DOESN'T, I MESSED THAT ONE UP PRETTY GOOD. CAN'T EVEN GET THE KID TO TALK TO ME ANYMORE. HE'S STUCK IN THERE FOR A FEW MORE MONTHS, AND HE'S GOT NOBODY. HE WON'T TAKE MY CALLS. I HOPE HIS MOM IS TALKING TO HIM AT LEAST. I THINK IT MIGHT BE TOO LATE FOR ME AND HIM. I MESSED UP TOO MANY TIMES. NOT THAT I'M A TOTAL SCREW UP. I'VE DONE SOME GOOD STUFF TOO! WHICH BRINGS ME TO 1995 AND HOW I MADE TWO GRAND BETTING ON THE OJ TRIAL.

creators and writers know that what's really funny, the real rivalry, is between Johnny and Daniel. So I think having the two women sort of team up to shine a light on how ridiculous the boys are—and were—is much more interesting to watch."

That doesn't stop fans from stacking Daniel's love interests against each other. "Ali is like the holy grail of all women," Henggeler says. "I get DMs constantly that are like, 'Yeah, you're cool. But you're not Ali,' and I'm like 'Thank you so much, always nice to meet a fan . . .' But I get it. Ali is the woman for both Daniel and Johnny who will always hold this very special place, and Amanda is the one who takes the air out of their tires."

Though fans were eager for an Ali-Daniel-Johnny reunion since *Cobra Kai* first started, bringing back the *Karate Kid* love interest wasn't just a ratings grab. Ali is the only person who can share firsthand insight into both men and their long-standing rivalry, and in doing so she helps move the story forward. After witnessing Daniel and Johnny relentlessly trading insults at the country club, she can't help but reveal her take on the feud: "This is exactly the problem," Ali says. "You both think there's only one side to the story . . . [but] there's three. There's your side, and your side, and then there is the truth. And the truth is, you guys are more alike than you want to admit. And maybe you recognize parts of yourselves in each other, and maybe you don't always like what you see." It represents the first time the senseis recognize their similarities and the potential in working together. And it doesn't come a moment too soon: later that same episode, after the fight at the LaRusso house, Johnny and Daniel decide the only way they can defeat Cobra Kai is if their dojos work together.

Despite dropping this necessary truth bomb, most of Ali's appearance on *Cobra Kai* is light and fun. Afternoons at Golf N' Stuff usually are. But in the world of *Cobra Kai*, no setting is immune to violence. In season three, the amusement park is the backdrop for one of the series' most merciless showdowns. It all starts when Hawk and some fellow Cobra Kais decide to make trouble in the arcade. After stealing a young girl's tickets and picking on Chris, the Miyagi-Do student who works at the ticket counter, the Cobra Kais sneak into the abandoned laser tag arena next door. When Chris calls for backup, Samantha, Demetri, and other Miyagi-Do students decide to show

INTERVIEW WITH

ELISABETH SHUE

What was it like returning to the Miyagi-verse after all these years?
It was like a high school reunion. Because *The Karate Kid* was my first film, I will always be more emotionally attached to it than some of my others. Filming with Ralph and Billy felt equally emotional. Especially saying goodbye to them.

How did it feel to reunite with Ralph and William, and act opposite them again?
First of all, I was reminded of what great actors they both are and how easily we reconnected on screen. Their lovely humanity and presence made it easy for me to inhabit Ali and instantly feel like no time had passed. I very much enjoyed watching them have to fight for my attention. It made me laugh and feel welcomed back into their story.

What do you think Ali was thinking seeing how little has changed between her two exes after all these years? Why was she the one to finally show them that they were more alike than different?
I never went to my high school reunion so this I guess will be the closest I ever come to one. It was comforting to see how little Ralph and Billy had changed. And from Ali's perspective, Johnny and Daniel were also exactly the same. Maybe a little more open to looking closer at themselves and maybe a little more willing to grow up. But not by much. That is the source of so much of *Cobra Kai*'s humor. And even though for a brief moment it appears they have listened to Ali's speech about being more alike than different, it does not lead to them becoming best friends; they go back to fighting each other again after I leave. They must like fighting an awful lot.

they can't be pushed around. But the laser tag confrontation doesn't go as they'd hoped: Hawk breaks Demetri's arm, and Samantha ends up hiding in a corner and having a panic attack when Tory comes looking for her. It's a critical moment for Samantha, who's suffering from post-traumatic stress disorder (PTSD) after Tory's attack on her with the spiked bracelet in the big high school fight. The laser tag scene was familiar territory for Mary Mouser, who also suffers from anxiety disorder and has experience with panic attacks. "Samantha's anxiety is a story line that I personally connected with, so I was really grateful to get to play that out on-screen," Mouser says. "To see her struggle with her post-traumatic stress and her trauma responses in general, I know that I, Mary, would have looked up to Sam so much."

> "Ali is like the holy grail of all women. I get DMs constantly that are like, 'Yeah, you're cool. But you're not Ali,' and I'm like 'Thank you so much, always nice to meet a fan . . .' But I get it. Ali is the woman for both Daniel and Johnny who will always hold this very special place, and Amanda is the one who takes the air out of their tires."
> —Courtney Henggeler

While Samantha's anxiety is a season-long story, Mouser says filming the panic attack, specifically, felt especially close to home. "I had my own experiences I was drawing from, and as an actor I usually prefer to do that," Mouser says. "I know everyone has their own methods, but for me it's crucial that I make a scene as true to my own personal experiences as I can. So I had to really dig in and ask myself, 'Okay, I have panic attacks, and everybody's panic attacks are different, so what are mine like?' It's a bizarre thing to observe about yourself when it's happening—like, 'Okay, I notice that I've been light-headed. I am feeling a tingling in my fingers. Interesting, I guess I'll take note of that for later, when I'm filming.'" Mouser says that getting herself into the right headspace to portray a panic attack almost induced her own emotional breakdown. "I'd been ramping myself up into this really heated, emotional place, so even doing the fight sequence that came before it felt different than usual. I got very frustrated because I couldn't get this one kick, and I ended up having to leave the room and scream."

Despite the difficulty and raw emotion wrapped up in this serious story, Mouser says it was an especially gratifying one to play out. "It's probably odd to use words like 'fun' and 'cool' when we are talking about PTSD and anxiety, but as an actor, portraying these difficult emotions is what I want to do, because there's so much good that can come out of a scene like that, and a story line like that." And despite battling anxiety that literally cripples the character throughout the season, Samantha ultimately comes out on top. "She didn't let the PTSD win," Mouser says. "That has been really cool."

SAM'S GUIDE TO A DRAMA-FREE LIFE

Life in the Valley can be . . . intense. And if you're not careful, you could find yourself in the middle of a massive karate war. It can happen to anyone. Or maybe just me. Anyway, if you want to avoid all the karate drama, here's how:

- Don't date. Seriously, every guy in the Valley is either in a dojo, about to join a dojo, or about to quit your dojo to join the evil dojo down the street. The best thing you can do is just stay away. Of course, if a guy's really special, sometimes there's nothing you can do—just because there's a karate war doesn't mean you can't be a normal teenager.

- Build bridges. Sometimes senseis get so caught up in their stupid rivalries that they forget what we're here for—to learn karate and stand up to bullies. Don't let their problems become your problems. Reach out to your friends in other dojos and teach the adults that people with different philosophies can still get along.

- Don't be a doormat. Not all differences can be overcome. If you don't stand up for yourself and hold your ground, people will walk all over you and make your life hell.

- Make friends with someone who knows how to deliver a nasty front wedgie. People will leave you alone.

07

THE ALL VALLEY TOURNAMENT

"WE NEED IT TO SHOW THE BULLIES OF THE WORLD WE'RE NOT AFRAID"

If you haven't figured this out by now, rumbles in the Valley are inevitable. Students from competing dojos can barely even be in the same room without someone throwing a punch. But when it comes to establishing true champions, there's only one place that matters: the All Valley Under 18 Karate Tournament. It's where Kreese first told Johnny to "sweep the leg" and where underdog Daniel LaRusso used his legendary crane kick to claim the first-place title. And thirty-four years later, it's where newcomer Miguel Diaz establishes himself as a fighter to be reckoned with. "When anyone thinks about *The Karate Kid*, the All Valley Tournament is at the top of their mind—two fighters putting it all on the line, on a mat, in front of the whole Valley," Josh Heald says. "It's the place where disputes are settled. If you have a disagreement in the Valley and you're under eighteen? Well, there's a place to bring that, and it's not the People's Court."

Though the tournament itself only appears in two of the series' first five seasons, its presence looms large. The first scene of the pilot is a flashback to the legendary 1984 finals battle between Johnny and Daniel, and as season one progresses, the audience is brought up to speed on the tournament's evolution in the decades since: attendance is dwindling, the 2017 event was plagued by a food poisoning incident thanks to a batch of bad corndogs, and the tournament committee's biggest controversy involves whether to change the mat color from red with a blue fist to blue with a gold fist. That is, until Johnny makes an appeal to overturn Cobra Kai's lifetime tournament ban, much to Daniel's dismay. Johnny's heartfelt plea to the board overseeing the event, which includes Daniel himself, is ultimately successful. In the season one finale, the all-new Cobra Kai dojo competes in the fiftieth annual tournament, with Miguel facing off against Robby Keene, then an unaffiliated student, in the finals.

In the wake of Miguel's victory, karate in the Valley undergoes a rebirth, and students at Cobra Kai, Miyagi-Do, and Eagle Fang are all excited to compete at the All Valley Tournament. That excitement is tempered momentarily when the tournament is canceled in the wake of the high school fight, and though Johnny, Daniel, and Kreese all appear in front of the city council in hopes of getting it reinstated, it's the testimonies of Samantha and Miguel that ultimately change the council's decision. "We don't need this tournament to do cool kicks or sell tickets, we need it to show the bullies of the world that we're not afraid," Miguel says. "It's called the All Valley because it's for everyone, to give everyone the chance to show what they can do, to fight, to become a champion. And we deserve that chance." At the end of season three, after the LaRusso home invasion pits the Eagle Fangs and Miyagi-Dos against the Cobra Kais, Johnny, Daniel, and Kreese come to an agreement: if Cobra Kai is defeated during the

BOARD MEETING MINUTES

Ron welcomes everyone to the All Valley Tournament Board meeting and offers congratulations all around on last year's massive success, in particular the outstanding performance by Carrie Underwood that will go down in Valley history

- George wonders how long Ron will be dining out on that

- Daryl points out that expectations for next year's tournament are higher than ever. And he's ready to step up. After all, there's only one man here with a record of revolutionary ideas

- George and Sue politely request that Daryl shut up about the blue mats already

- Gavin asks if they can get to the matter at hand and discuss snack vendors for the next tournament

- Sue reminds everyone of the great corndog debacle of 2017

- George says that wasn't his fault

- Ron says yes it was, how could he have forgotten to check the health department rating?

- Sue claims that she wasn't trying to blame anyone, but if she had been, then yes, it was George's fault, and maybe someone else should take responsibility for the vendors

- George asks Sue why she's so cranky and if "it's that time of the month"

- Sue throws an unidentified object, possibly a stapler, at George

- Gavin requests that everyone just calm down, please, for the love of God

- Daryl thinks Gavin doesn't understand the stakes here. This is karate in the Valley, and anyone who's calm doesn't care enough

- Gavin leaves, shouting an expletive and calling everyone power-mad, karate-obsessed lunatics

- Ron, George, Daryl, and Sue wonder what that guy's problem is

upcoming All Valley tournament, Kreese will leave town and Cobra Kai will shut down for good.

While the All Valley informs plenty of *Cobra Kai* story lines in the first three seasons, it's not until season four that the tournament takes center stage. The matches make up the entirety of the season's final two episodes, but all ten installments revolve around the iconic tournament—the training, the student recruiting, even the sensei pairings, which pit Johnny and Daniel against Kreese and his old war buddy and *The Karate Kid Part III* villain, Terry Silver. And just as karate in the Valley has boomed in popularity, so too has the tournament itself. By season four, the event looks less like a dull amateur exhibition and more like a WWE match, with colored strobe lights, smoke machines, screaming fans, and a surprise musical performance from country superstar and *American Idol* winner Carrie Underwood, who covers *Survivor* single "Moment of Truth,"

> "It's called the All Valley because it's for everyone, to give everyone the chance to show what they can do, to fight, to become a champion. And we deserve that chance."
> —Miguel Diaz

originally written for *The Karate Kid*. The format sees a more substantive evolution, too. Halfway through *Cobra Kai*'s fourth season, the tournament committee votes to modernize the event and respond to karate's newfound popularity with two sweeping changes: a newly added skills competition, which showcases students' work with katas and martial arts weapons like kamas, sais, and bo staffs, and a second tournament bracket for girls. Instead of a single All Valley champion, there will now be two, and the combined scores of all three competitions will determine the overall Grand Champion dojo. It is, as Daniel LaRusso tells his students, "a whole new ballgame." (Johnny's take isn't quite as elegant: "Skills competitions? Bullshit! Kata isn't karate, it's dancing! And what's this crap about a girls' division? I thought they wanted equality? They oughta man up and take a punch like everyone else.")

Training for every season can be intense, and the young actors in *Cobra Kai* say season four and the tournament episodes required even more demanding physical work. Despite each actor being supplied with a stunt double, they all

TERRY SILVER

DOJO: Cobra Kai

ALLY: John Kreese (former)

NEMESES: Daniel LaRusso, Nariyoshi Miyagi (former)

CHARACTER PHILOSOPHY: "If they think you're weak—
that's when you can surprise them with your strength."

try to do as many of their own stunts as possible. "I'd say I get to do around ninety percent of my stunts," Xolo Maridueña says. "The only stuff I don't do are the moves where they're like, 'You could actually hurt yourself here.' Stuff like falling from a balcony or getting thrown into a trophy case. And I really believe we are given that freedom because we, as actors, have such great relationships with the stunt coordinators—they trust us and can say, 'Hey, we know what you can and can't do, so let's make sure we're being safe and putting a lot of practice in.'"

Having the actors in their own fight scenes makes the show feel more authentic for the audience, too. "It's so much better when, as a viewer, you're like 'Wait a second!' and you pause the screen and it's like 'That's really them!'" Maridueña says. "It's been such a special experience. Honestly, I'm a little bummed out for whenever I have another project with stunts, because I think this is the exception, not the norm."

Jacob Bertrand agrees. "They train us to be able to do as much of the action as we can, and if we're able to do it, they'll let us do it," he says. "I really love that philosophy. I loved the season two fight in the woods with Xolo, because it was pretty technical and it was a really hard day and ninety-nine

THOMAS IAN GRIFFITH (TERRY SILVER)

What was it like returning to the Miyagi-verse after all these years?

A bit surreal. *Karate Kid III* was my first film role. John Avildsen took a chance on an unknown New York actor and, along with screenwriter Robert Mark Kamen, created this over the top, archetypal villain that gave the franchise a bolt of new energy. To be able to go back thirty years later and reprise that role was not something I could've ever imagined back then. What the creators of *Cobra Kai* wisely did was make Terry Silver a much more complex, multi-dimensional character, one the audience can relate to because they understand his psychological journey. For me, bringing the new version of Terry to light brought the *Karate Kid* experience full circle and was very rewarding creatively.

How did it feel to reunite with Martin, and act opposite him again?

It was great to see the OG gang again—Ralph, Billy and, of course, Marty. To be able to pick up where we left off, only this time armed with thirty years of life experience, I knew right away this was going to be something special.

Why do you think Terry was ultimately unable to resist the pull back to Kreese and Cobra Kai?

Loyalty. Terry was fiercely loyal to Kreese. When we first meet Terry in the series, he has surrounded himself with love, art, music. And those beautiful distractions have kept his demons at bay . . . until Kreese shows up. Kreese knows what buttons to push. Terry initially wants nothing to do with him, but the love he has for his oldest friend in the world is so strong Terry can't turn his back on him. But when Terry realizes Kreese is taking advantage of that loyalty, all bets are off.

Now that we know more of Terry Silver's backstory, how do you think he was affected by his war experience, and how does that inform his action today?

You have to find commonality with and understanding of every character you play. I was too young to have experienced Vietnam firsthand, but I understand the darkness that haunts Terry. It's put him on a path of survival. It's also given him an unquenchable drive to succeed—it's why he's such a successful businessman, why he's such an accomplished pianist, why he's willing to go to extremes for what he believes is right. He's trying to stay one step ahead of his demons. In Vietnam he faced his greatest fear—cowardice—and it consumed him. That's why he's so committed to passing the Cobra Kai way on to the next generation so they're strong enough to conquer their own fears, no matter what the situation.

percent of that fight is us, with the exception of a move we just didn't have time to learn. But I was so proud of how it came out." One of Gianni DeCenzo's favorite action-packed scenes is the LaRusso home invasion, which occurs at the end of season three. "It was all one take for the most part," he says. "We had to choreograph so many different smaller fights just to make the world look real. At one point, about halfway through the fight, I fall onto a chair, and then I actually had to take that chair and drag it behind the cameraman as he was walking around so that he didn't trip, and then put it back into place and return to the acting world. There were a lot of moving pieces, it was like we are dancing. Like the Sharks versus the Jets."

West Side Story references aside, preparing one's own stunts means serious training, and most of the actors arrived with no prior experience—though some did take martial arts when they were kids. Bertrand got to a purple belt in karate and also took Jiujitsu, which he says he "pretty much just used on my brother when we would wrestle"; DeCenzo took Tae Kwon Do and Krav Maga; Maridueña did a couple years of karate starting when he was in kindergarten. But they all say those early classes didn't do much to prepare them for the level of action involved in filming *Cobra Kai*. Some of them didn't even know, when they auditioned for their roles, that their characters would be fighting. When Bertrand first read for his role, "there was no Hawk, there was

only Eli," he says. And Peyton List, who had never taken a martial arts class, says her audition breakdown (the brief description of the project an actor gets before an audition) didn't even mention that stunts would be required. "I was definitely not prepared," she says. Luckily her stunt double, Jahnel Curfman, was also one of the show's stunt coordinators. "She just threw me right in and started training me," List says. "She was like, 'You can do it, throw some punches, let's go,' and she really coached me throughout all of season two, which was my first season on the show. When we got to the end of that season, after we'd filmed all the fighting, Jahnel started crying. She was like 'I'm just so proud of you,' and honestly that was the biggest compliment I could have received, because she was like my very own sensei."

(The one actor who did have an extensive karate background? Owen Morgan, who plays Eagle Fang fighter Bert. He may be known in the dojo for his small stature, but in real life his family runs a karate school, and Morgan achieved his black belt in 2019. He even shared a pic with his real-life senseis on his Instagram, noting that "nine years have led up to this, and I couldn't be more proud!")

In the early days of filming, the top-billed actors' specific training regimens varied depending on the character. "Our stunt coordinator for the first three seasons, Hiro Koda, made it clear that if Daniel was going to be teaching a whole different style of karate than Johnny, then the young actors should be trained in different styles, too, because we're not all going to look the same on the mat," Maridueña says. Miguel's fighting (and

Maridueña's training) comes from Tang Soo Do, a Korean martial art based on karate that Johnny uses in the original *Karate Kid* (and which Terry Silver brings back in controversial form in season five). Bertrand, on the other hand, says much of Hawk's more aggressive style is based on Muay Thai, or "Thai boxing," thanks in large part to his tutelage under John Kreese.

The inclusion of more characters naturally means the inclusion of more fighting styles. "In season four, a lot of thought went into my stance, the way I move, the way I attack," says Tanner Buchanan, who plays Robby. By the end of season four, Robby has studied extensively under both Daniel and Kreese, so Buchanan wanted his action sequences to reflect that. "I had long conversations with our fight coordinator, Don Lee, to make sure there was a major progression in Robby's fighting style." The same was true for Mary Mouser's Samantha, who spends much of season four learning from Johnny Lawrence, and, in the season's finale fight, combines Eagle Fang's and Miyagi-Do's styles to create something all her own. "'Samantha Style,' that's what everyone was calling it," Mouser says. "In that final fight, there's a

KARATE CHAMPIONSHIPS

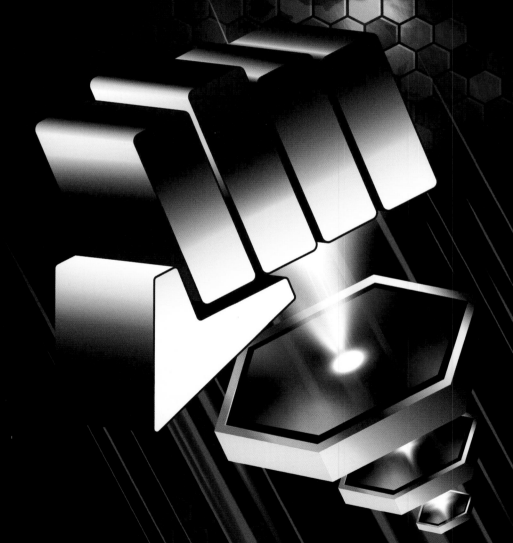

ALL VALLEY SPORTS ARENA

51ˢᵗ ALL VALLEY
TOURNAMENT PROGRAM

For more than half a century, karate dojos across the San Fernando Valley have come face-to-face on the All Valley Tournament mat for a taste of glory and the championship title. This year, the tournament makes history by adding a skills competition and splitting competitors into boys' and girls' competitions. May the best dojo win!

FEATURING A SURPRISE MUSICAL PERFORMANCE!

COMPETING DOJOS
**ALL STAR KARATE, COBRA KAI, CUTTING EDGE KARATE,
EAGLE FANG, LOCUST VALLEY, MIYAGI-DO KARATE, TOPANGA KARATE**

SKILLS COMPETITIONS
**KATAS, BOARD BREAKING,
WEAPONS DISPLAY (KAMAS, BO STAFF, SAIS, KATANA)**

QUARTERFINALISTS

BOYS

- DIAZ
- KASTELLANOS
- KEENE
- MOSKOWITZ
- PARK
- PAYNE
- POST
- ROBSON

GIRLS

- ELSWITH
- GONZALES
- KRUPA
- LARUSSO
- LEE
- MURPHY
- NICHOLS
- POWERS

moment where Samantha does make a very distinctive turn in her style and our stunt team worked really closely with me on that—we came up with this hybrid of one hand in a very Eagle Fang position and the other one in a very Miyagi-Do position, and my stance was such that my weight was placed in not a particularly Miyagi-esque karate stance, but not particularly Eagle Fang. Those details, to me, are cool, because it shows how every fighter can have her own distinctive style based on her own distinctive influences. There is no one right way."

But not every character benefited from the combination of teachers. By the end of season four, Miguel is most definitely struggling to find himself, on and off the mat. "I think the fact that Miguel has a little bit of experience with Kreese and gets some experience with Daniel in season four, what we see is that he is a jack of all trades but a master of none," Maridueña says. "He has bits and pieces of all these different dojos and is trying to find the balance between when to use which one, and I think that practice is difficult for him."

Because season four is so fight-heavy, anchored by the technicality of the tournament episodes, training for all the young actors was turned up a notch. Any day a member of the student cast wasn't filming, they trained for two to four hours, doing a combination of group training (including learning specific punches and kicks), individual training with their stunt doubles, circuit training, stretching, and choreography. "The worst is when we have to do HIIT [high-intensity interval training] or a bunch of push-ups, a bunch of sit-ups, a bunch of squats—that stuff is so rough," Bertrand says. "But even when we're home, we'll be stretching or helping each other stretch, and it's because we love being able to do this stuff, so we want to do everything we can to continue doing it ourselves. It's pretty fun, actually, it's like being on a sports team."

The All Valley episodes took two weeks to film, and the days were long and draining, List says. "The endurance we needed for those two weeks of filming? We were up at four a.m. and we weren't back in bed until eleven, but we were just going for it, because the whole season built up to the All Valley. All the training we had done all season, it all came to this," she says.

Heald, who directed both tournament episodes, joined Mouser and List in front of the on-set crowd for their final prefight warmup with stunt coordinator Don Lee, and says that ten-minute stretch alone was a workout. "I'm still

DON LEE

I n season four, Don Lee joined the *Cobra Kai* crew as fight coordinator, choreographing some of the series' most memorable face-offs. Lee, who has worked on movies like *Pirates of the Caribbean* and *Daredevil*, is a longtime martial artist himself. In fact, he owned a dojo before becoming a stuntman. Here, he gives a glimpse behind the scenes of the All Valley's most epic matches, the prom night throwdown, and training fighters from three different dojos.

Obviously, different senseis in the Miyagi-verse have different styles, so their students fight differently. How do you train the cast differently, or choreograph differently, based on their dojo?

We start by talking to the writers to understand the backstory—we always want to stay true to what is created in the writers' room. Because of that, we keep Miyagi-Do very Okinawan style—traditional, self-defense based. Then we keep Cobra Kai very kind of Tae Kwon Do—that strike-first, strike-hard element. And when Johnny Lawrence breaks away from that for Eagle Fang, we made that Tae Kwon Do–inspired, with some Tang Soo Do and some "Billy Badass" mixed in . . . that's what we call it. That's the element that William Zabka, as Johnny, puts into it.

But it also changes from character to character. Samantha, for example, she has the true martial arts lineage. So there's a lot of fundamentals we put into her repertoire—you can see it in her stances, or how powerful she is on the basics. But then there's Hawk: he has this mixture of having been trained in Cobra Kai and now being in Miyagi-Do, so we had to weave that story element into it. That idea of "Well, my instincts would be to strike first, but I can't do that, because I'm in Miyagi-Do, so how do I find a balance?"

It's also important to consider the actors themselves, because we always want to train to their strengths. We want to give them the moves that will make them look good, because by season four, especially the end of season four, every one of them should look like they know martial arts.

Some of the most dynamic fight scenes take place off the mat. In season four, there's an especially memorable fight after the prom, when Robby and Tory take on Miguel and Samantha. What goes into creating a fight like that?

Emotion! A lot of emotion-driven action. We really had to collaborate with Jon, Josh, and Hayden on that fight and make sure it hit every story beat they had, but we also wanted it to catch people off guard. Obviously, the tension between the girls had been building all season long, so when Tory delivers the line, "I don't take orders from tiny, little bitches," well, Samantha had just had enough. And it's this important moment when Samantha's character is tired of being on defense. So the Eagle Fang comes out of her and she ends up striking first. So that was fun, to have the tables turn, where it's not always Tory starting it between them. And then we wanted to make sure it's a fun fight. The gloves were off, so to speak. It's not a tournament fight, there's no, "I score a point and then there's a break and you go to your side, I go to my side." Then there was the final element to it, which was the fact that the girls are wearing dresses. They couldn't wear knee pads without them showing, they couldn't put pads on their arms. The only padding in that fight was the high-dense foam we used for the concrete floor.

Season four also added weapons and a skills competition to the All Valley Tournament. What was that training like?

I was so happy that the writers put that in there because growing up in sport karate, these were the skills competitions that we did. This is part of the process of competing. And it gave our actors a different world to learn versus just fighting. This is performing, and there's a reason why they are called martial *arts*. It's a form of expression. There is a performance element to it.

It was funny, too, because one of the first movies I worked on was training Jennifer Garner on the sais for the movie *Daredevil*. And then I trained her on *Elektra*. So when I started working with Mary Mouser on the sais I was like, this is the weapon I trained Jennifer Garner on. And, of course, Mary was like "I love Jennifer Garner," so there are a few beats in Samantha's kata that were in the original *Daredevil* movie—a little nod to that.

Still, the fights were the highlight of season four's All Valley episodes. And there were so many! How did you do it all?

There was a total of sixty fights we had to choreograph and teach. Six-zero! There were the main fights, but there were also the fights in the background, and the fights during the montage when Carrie Underwood was performing. All these little fights that are five, six, seven beats. Whereas the Hawk-Robby fight, which, in the story, is the longest round without scoring a point—that fight was 235 beats long. And the female championship was 171 beats. It's a lot! The hardest thing about point fighting is that, if you make contact, that's a point. So we had to be really intricate for the choreography. Plus, it's really important as a stunt coordinator to make sure that you don't fall into a rut where all the fights start to look the same. That's when viewers start to get fight fatigue, and that's the last thing we want. There has to be a sense of character with all these things.

With all this fighting, how do you decide when to bring in stunt doubles and when to use the actors?
Sometimes it's just about how game they are, but a lot of times it's more about a risk assessment. Let's say we're working with Jacob [Bertrand], who is super talented, but we've already been working for four hours and we have two more to go. We may be working on a spring floor that has mats and is soft, but we still have to make a risk assessment as coordinators—is it worth risking injury? We also consider where the camera is focused—if we are just seeing the back of someone's head and it's a really tricky move, then it makes sense to give the actor a break and put in a double. But we are lucky, because every actor really *wants* to do their stunts, and I'm not used to working with a cast like that. It's awesome, because the audience, they want to see the actors. And everyone—the adults and the "kids"—are equally game. These guys pour their heart and soul into all of it.

exhausted," he says. "What they did to get loose before the cameras even rolled felt like a personal training session."

That level of training was also necessary to give some of the actors the physical transformation that would accompany their character's increased dojo time. Buchanan said he added at least an hour of individual training three to four times a week so his body would accurately reflect the amount of training Robby was doing, and while all the fighters go through a clear evolution as their karate skills advance, Buchanan's particular dedication is showcased in the season finale fight between Hawk and Robby, where both students rip off their uniforms and fight shirtless in an especially '80s-esque moment. Think Axl Rose and Billy Idol, if they traded in their microphones for karate gis.

For Mary Mouser, the training that started as part of her acting gig has morphed into a lifelong habit. "I train in my off season—usually doing Muay Thai—as much as I possibly can," she says. "It's bizarre to me, because I used to be the kid who got a note to get out of PE." For season four's All Valley Tournament, Mouser's training evolved to include the sai, a traditional Okinawan three-pronged dagger, which she needed to master in order to perform Samantha's kata in the skills competition. Mouser says she had the weapons

"in my hand, every single day, for a minimum of two hours a day, in addition to the rest of my karate training." After all that work, Mouser has "gotten really into weaponry. I love the artistry of it and the history of it. I've learned how to use the sai, how to use the bo staff, and I picked up a few pieces of katana [a Japanese sword] from Peyton, who used it for Tory's skills competition. It's really taken over so many aspects of my mental and physical health."

But the most rewarding aspect of the All Valley wasn't showing off her flying tornado kick or rocking her skills with the sais, Mouser says. It was being represented in that final tournament match. "I'll admit, when I learned they were splitting up the tournament and pitting girls against girls, guys against guys, I was nervous. I was worried that the girls' bracket would become a throwaway," she says. "So when I first read the finale script, and saw that the women would be fighting the deciding fight at the end of the season, I cried. The fact that our fight got to be the one that determined which dojo came out on top—I was so grateful."

List agrees wholeheartedly. "It was the most fun I have ever had on the show," she says. "To be in that black gi, and be up on the All Valley floor . . . it was completely surreal."

After the heated battle between Robby and Hawk, everything comes down to one final fight: the girls division championship. Tory and Samantha face off in an epic showdown, with the winner's dojo crowned Grand Champion. It's Cobra Kai vs. Miyagi-Do, just as it was a generation ago, when Johnny and Daniel faced off in the very same arena. And while the energy in the room—and the magnitude of the fight—is the same as it was all those years back, the outcome is different: Tory lands the deciding victory (with, yes, a little help from a bribed referee), and her fellow Cobra Kais immediately embrace their new champion. The future of the dojo was at stake, and now Miyagi-Do and Eagle Fang are expected to shut down their operations.

But that's not the only outcome the *Cobra Kai* crew filmed. Because of the size of the tournament crowd and the number of extras, the creators wanted to protect against the possibility of spoilers getting leaked ahead of the season's release, so they filmed an alternate ending, this one with Samantha winning the fight and getting hoisted up onto Daniel's and Johnny's shoulders.

Despite her victory, Peyton List says the best part of filming the All Valley episodes wasn't the fighting or the spotlight on her character or her long-awaited hero moment. It was the camaraderie, and the realization that *Cobra*

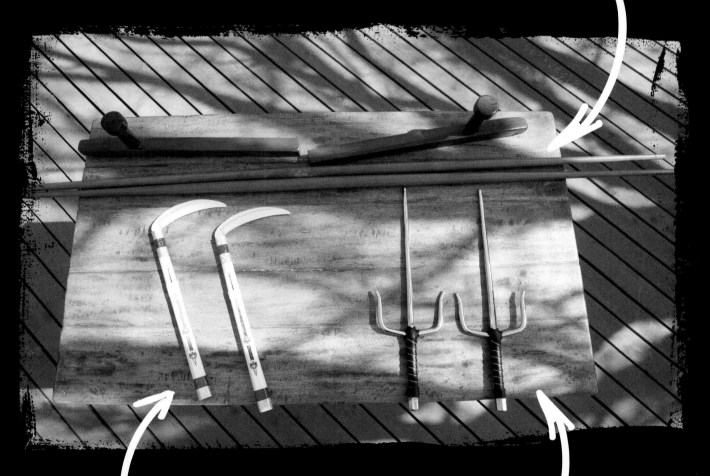

Bo Staff

Kamas

Sais

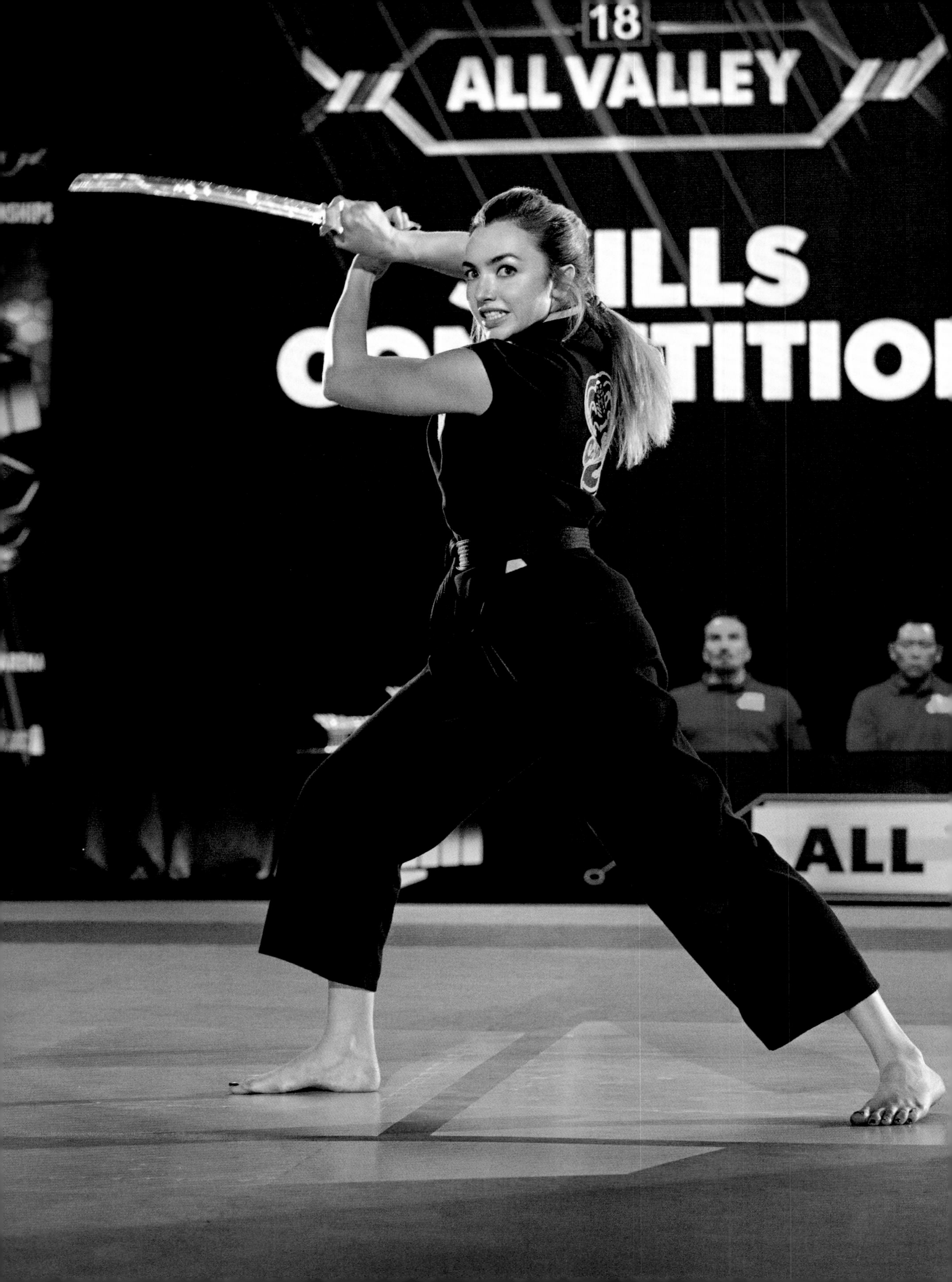
18
ALL VALLEY
ALL

Kai is a legacy more than a TV show. "I had so much time on the sidelines with Martin Kove and Thomas Ian Griffith and Ralph Macchio and William Zabka. William's kids even came to watch!" she says. (They can be seen briefly in the season finale, walking behind Johnny after the tournament, when he's saying goodbye to Carmen.) "To be able to talk to them on the sidelines for hours, like we were at a real tournament, and ask 'What's this like for you? Is it so trippy?' It was just so much fun getting to pick their brains about the whole thing. And seeing William's son—who looks exactly like him—watching his dad, it's like this whole world keeps getting bigger, and getting passed down, and that's pretty cool."

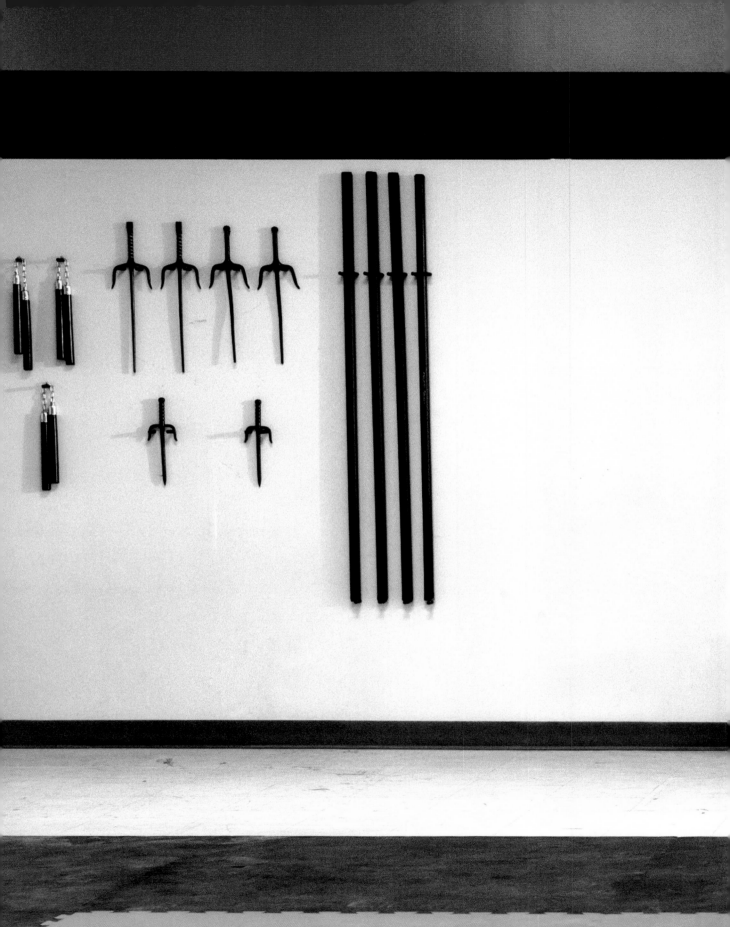

Special thanks to Mattea Greene!

Safety Disclaimer: Don't try these moves at home!

HarperCollins books may be purchased for educational, business, or sales promotional use.
For information, please email the Special Markets Department at SPsales@harpercollins.com.

FIRST EDITION

Designed by Angie Boutin

Background papers, torn edges, paint graphics, doodles, and cassette tape cases (p. 145)
© stock.adobe.com; © shutterstock

Library of Congress Cataloging-in-Publication Data has been applied for.

ISBN 978-0-06-321785-0

22 23 24 25 26   WOR   10 9 8 7 6 5 4 3 2 1

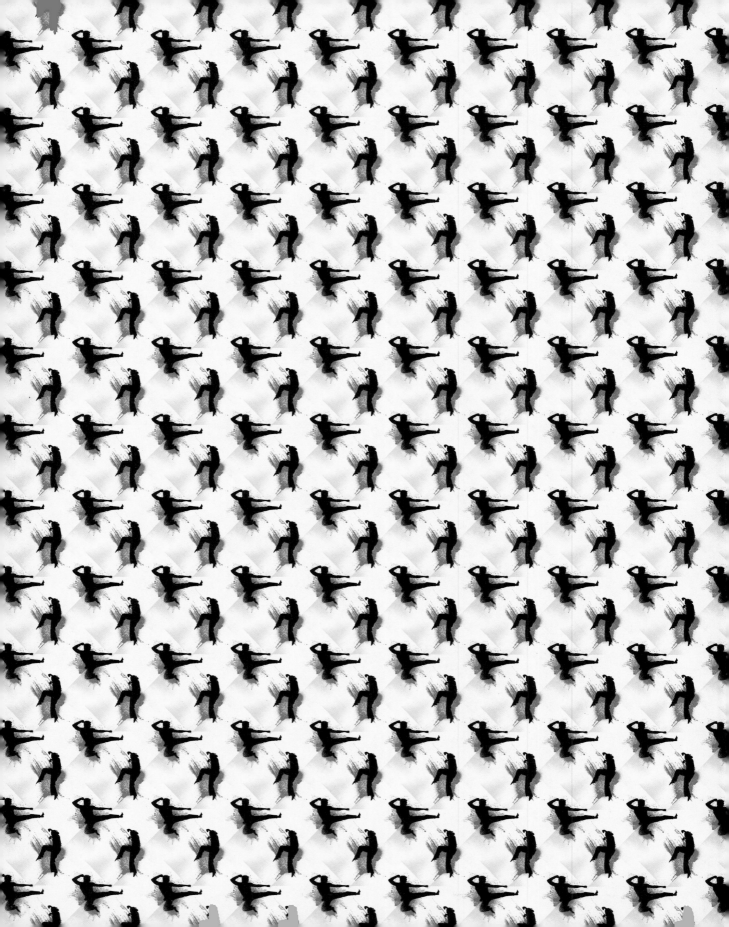